"In his brilliant and highly influential work, Philip Bromberg wrote from his deeply personal immersion in clinical process, not from the intention to create a systematic theory. This approach, while it led Bromberg to create some of the most gripping prose in the psychoanalytic literature, can make the systematic under-standing of his body of work elusive. Now, in this highly illumi-nating introduction by Bass and Ceccoli, we have for the first time an overview of Bromberg's work, presented in a way that, while preserving its 'feel,' systematically teaches the ideas and lays out the history of their development. This book immediately becomes the place to start if you are beginning to read Bromberg; but it is just as profitable for readers who have read Bromberg for years. I knew the man well and have been deeply influenced by him; and even with that background, I learned a great deal from reading this text. I recommend it highly."

Donnel B. Stern, William Alanson White Institute, NYU Postdoctoral Program in Psychotherapy and Psychoanalysis

"Ceccoli and Bass have poured their hearts and minds into this exploration of the work of Philip Bromberg. It's not just the ideas of Bromberg they convey, but the experience of sitting with him and soaking in his sensibilities, an experience to savor. With great clinical agility and nuance, they have captured many of the essen-ces of what Bromberg embraced in his inimitable casually intense regard for what he could sense was hidden in people below their own radar. Using clinical vignettes and cogently collecting and elaborating on Bromberg's most salient contributions to psycho-analysis, they have rekindled, for me, the light that was Philip. Their writing is a gift for all of us."

Richard A. Chefetz, MD, Washington-Baltimore Center for Psychoanalysis, author of *Intensive Psychotherapy for Persistent Dissociative Processes: The Fear of Feeling Real*

"Bass and Ceccoli deftly capture the essence of the 'Brombergian' ethos as they transport the reader into the felt experience of Philip Bromberg's remarkable clinical thinking. From the quotidian to the sublime, the authors harness their understanding of Bromberg's insights into self-state-sharing and the unparalleled importance of a clinical encounter that feels personal and real, while also knowing that in the clinical dyad, this must be a two-way street. With exquisite clarity, Bass and Ceccoli explicate and expand Bromberg's contributions to unpacking the complex internal and relational consequences of developmental trauma as it influences dissociation, multiplicity, and the importance of a dyadic self-state model in transforming enactments from therapeutic impasse to therapeutic action. Readers cannot help but become immersed, participating with the authors in an emergent creative process that, in its ingenuity and creativity, would be right after Bromberg's heart. In addition to offering a profound contribution in their own right, the authors give of us the gift of bringing Bromberg near. One can easily imagine him wanting to ask the reader 'What was it like for YOU reading this book?' And as you contemplate your answer, perhaps you'll feel Bromberg not only 'standing in the spaces' next to you, but also sitting with you as you spontaneously savor every morsel."

Jean Petrucelli, PhD, Training & Supervising Analyst, William Alanson White Institute, and editor of the book *Body-States: Interpersonal/Relational Perspectives in the Treatment of Eating Disorders*

"This truly is the book I would have wished for in training. As the authors note, Bromberg's articles and books are readily available. What has not existed until now is an overview and synthesis of his work in one highly readable volume. By citing the ways in which this beloved teacher and supervisor continues to influence Bass and Ceccoli, the reader is invited to discover their own Philip Bromberg. In that respect, as Bromberg himself might have noted, this volume is an enactment of his most firmly held belief; psychoanalysis is best understood, practiced and learned as a subjective and intersubjective venture."

Dr. Steven Kuchuck, author of *The Relational Revolution in Psychoanalysis and Psychotherapy*, former president of IARPP, and editor of the Routledge Relational Perspectives Book series

"In this enlightening study, Bass and Ceccoli testify to the profound influence of Philip Bromberg on their analytic thinking and on that of generations of students and colleagues. This is an engaging and lucid exploration of the complex elements bridged in Bromberg's theory and practice. For all who are interested in the functioning of the mind and in the collisions and negotiations of the therapeutic relationship – both experienced clinicians and the humanist reading public – it offers a valuable new mapping of Bromberg's achievement."

Avivah Zornberg, author of *The Murmuring Deep: Reflections on the Biblical Unconscious*

"This important book conveys Philip Bromberg's essential version of relational psychoanalysis in all its unique wisdom and erudition, tenderness and self-reflection. It is a work of love for the practice of psychoanalysis that will inspire and enlighten."

Jessica Benjamin, author of *Beyond Doer and Done To*

Philip Bromberg

This important volume offers the first introduction to Philip Bromberg and his work, introducing the reader to his ground-breaking contributions to clinical psychoanalysis.

Anthony Bass and Velleda C. Ceccoli draw on their experience as Bromberg's students, supervisees, colleagues, and friends to outline and elaborate his key ideas and their applications to therapeutic work. Considering Bromberg's importance in the field of interpersonal and relational psychoanalysis and psychotherapy, they draw on his theories of dissociation, enactment, and multiplicity to show the importance of self-states for both the therapist and patient within a therapeutic setting.

This book will be of great interest to both psychoanalysts and psychotherapists, as well as students in mental health professions and analytic candidates.

Anthony Bass is an Adjunct Associate Professor at the NYU Postdoctoral Program in Psychoanalysis and Psychotherapy and a Training and Supervising Analyst at the Columbia University Center for Psychoanalytic Training and Research in the department of Psychiatry. He is in private practice in New York City, USA.

Velleda C. Ceccoli is Adjunct Clinical Associate Professor and Supervisor in the Postdoctoral Program for Psychoanalysis and Psychotherapy at New York University and faculty at The Stephen Mitchell Relational Study Center. She is a psychologist and psychoanalyst in private practice in New York USA.

Routledge Introductions to Contemporary Psychoanalysis

Series Editor: Aner Govrin
Executive Editor: Yael Peri Herzovich

For more information about this series, please visit: www.routledge.com/Routledge-Introductions-to-Contemporary-Psychoanalysis/book-series/ICP

Philip Bromberg

A Contemporary Introduction

Anthony Bass and
Velleda C. Ceccoli

LONDON AND NEW YORK

Designed cover image: © Michal Heiman, Asylum 1855–2020, The Sleeper (video, psychoanalytic sofa and Plate 34), exhibition view, Herzliya Museum of Contemporary Art, 2017

First published 2026
by Routledge
4 Park Square, Milton Park, Abingdon, Oxon OX14 4RN

and by Routledge
605 Third Avenue, New York, NY 10158

Routledge is an imprint of the Taylor & Francis Group, an informa business

British Library Cataloguing-in-Publication Data
A catalogue record for this book is available from the British Library

ISBN: 978-1-032-46474-9 (hbk)
ISBN: 978-1-032-43847-4 (pbk)
ISBN: 978-1-003-38185-3 (ebk)

DOI: 10.4324/9781003381853

Typeset in Times New Roman
by Taylor & Francis Books

For Laura—A. B.
For Philip—V. C.

Contents

Series Editor's Preface

Routledge Introductions to Contemporary Psychoanalysis is one of the most prominent psychoanalytic publishing ventures of our day. The series' aim is to become an encyclopedia of psychoanalysis, with each entry given its own book.

This comprehensive series illuminates the intricate landscape of psychoanalytic theory and practice. In this collection of concise yet illuminating volumes, we delve into the influential figures, groundbreaking concepts, and transformative theories that shape the contemporary psychoanalytic landscape.

At the heart of each volume lies a commitment to clarity, accessibility, and depth. Our expert authors, renowned scholars and practitioners in their respective fields, guide readers through the complexities of psychoanalytic thought with precision and enthusiasm. Whether you are a seasoned psychoanalyst, a student eager to explore the field, or a curious reader seeking insight into the human psyche, our series offers a wealth of knowledge and insight.

Each volume serves as a gateway into a specific aspect of psychoanalytic theory and practice. From the pioneering works of Sigmund Freud to the innovative contributions of modern theorists such as Antonino Ferro and Michal Eigen, our series covers a diverse range of topics, including seminal figures, key concepts, and emerging trends. Whether you are interested in classical psychoanalysis, object relations theory, or the intersection of neuroscience and psychoanalysis, you will find a wealth of resources within our collection.

One of the hallmarks of our series is its interdisciplinary approach. While rooted in psychoanalytic theory, our volumes draw upon insights from psychology, philosophy, sociology, and other disciplines to offer a holistic understanding of the human mind and its complexities.

Each volume in the series is crafted with the reader in mind, balancing scholarly rigor with engaging prose. Whether you are embarking on your journey into psychoanalysis or seeking to deepen your understanding of specific topics, our series provides a clear and comprehensive roadmap.

Moreover, our series is committed to fostering dialogue and debate within the psychoanalytic community. Each volume invites readers to critically engage with the material, encouraging reflection, discussion, and further exploration.

We invite you to join us on this journey of discovery as we explore the ever-evolving landscape of psychoanalysis.

Aner Govrin

Forewords

When Tony first asked me to collaborate with him on a book about Philip Bromberg's work I was thrilled at the thought of it. I had been leading a study group called *The Bromberg Variations* for about two years, our mission was to read everything that Philip had published in chronological order. Then I wondered, what would Philip say if I told him that Tony and I were going to write a book about his work?

His voice came through loud and clear:

"Are you sure you want to do that?!"
"Who would want to read it?!"

There are many such dialogues with Philip in my head—most of them arrive unannounced. After working with Philip for 28 years in supervision, thinking with him about clinical work, theory, human motivation, and what is meaningful about psychoanalytic psychotherapy, Philip sneaks into my mind, often guiding my work and influencing my thoughts and my writing. In a way it is a continuation of a dialogue begun when I was a candidate and took his class at NYU Postdoc, which then led me to be in group supervision with him until he retired. Our friendship grew out of our work together and remained extremely important and central in my life. Philip taught me to be wary of technique and curious about theory, he taught me to exercise my analytic voice and use it with forceful vulnerability. And so those dialogues continue, and the writing of this book calls them forth anew.

Many of our colleagues have similar experiences of Philip. I think that each of us has a singular Philip, our very own Philip who influenced us in particular ways through our relationship with him. My Philip taught me to be *really real* (as in *The Velveteen Rabbit* REAL) in relationship, and to trust the strength of a relationship based on authenticity. For Philip it was all about the relationship, and how reciprocal it was. He knew that a person could not transcend his or her dissociation without the presence of another who could recognize their own and be willing to dialogue about it. His interest was on how *real* we could allow ourselves to be while addressing not only the parts of ourselves that we know and are relatively comfortable with; he wanted to know the parts that we might prefer to have nothing to do with. His belief in multiplicity was present in all of his relationships: internal, external, professional, and personal.

Philip had something akin to X-ray vision, and an incredible sensitivity for those self-states that liked to hide (thus his interest in Sullivan's not me self-states), AND for those parts of the self that have a different story to tell. *That* was the story that Bromberg was interested in, the story that he built a theory on, so that as clinicians we might have a way to help our patients finally find and put words to what was "sorta" known and definitely felt.

As a candidate at the William Alanson White Institute, Bromberg was already mixing it up with different psychoanalytic theories, pushing the boundaries so as to make theory useable clinically. As an interpersonal psychoanalyst he was a devotee of Sullivan, yet his interest in working with character disorders led him to the work of the British Object Relations school in order to find a way to identify, name, and treat the regression he observed in his consulting room. This was the first of many integrations of theory into his interpersonal background. The development of his ideas on multiplicity and dissociation then led him to the field of traumatology, the study of dissociative disorders, neuroscience, cognitive science, and back to his Sullivanian roots and relational psychoanalysis.

"Can you get all of this into a book??????" I can hear him asking. We are going to try …

Velleda C. Ceccoli

* * * *

Philip Bromberg and I began a conversation about psychoanalysis and our experiences practicing it in 1988. He was my last supervisor when I was in psychoanalytic training in the 1980s at the NYU Postdoctoral Program. I continued speaking with Philip about my work, and everything else, until the time of his death. It had been 32 years. I remember the first time we spoke. He had a distinctive New York/Brooklyn inflected voice, and a full big frequent laugh.. When I got wind of the fact that he was joining the newly forming relational faculty at NYU, spearheaded by his old friends from the WA White Institute, my new friends, Stephen Mitchell and Emanuel Ghent, it was a bit like the Seven Samurai, with Stephen and Emanuel gathering together the best group of analysts they could find to take on both the Freudian and Interpersonal establishment at NYU to bring the newly forming Relational Perspective into being. I had long admired Bromberg's paper, Interpersonal Psychoanalysis and Regression, a forerunner of what was about to become known as relational psychoanalysis. The paper predated the emergence of the relational turn in psychoanalysis of which he would be an integral part. It presaged the brilliantly scholarly work of Greenberg and Mitchell (1983) and Mitchell (1988, 1991, 1993, 2000) that finally put a relational conflict model forward as an alternative to a classical drive conflict model in its artful and at the time radical way of combining currents in interpersonal psychoanalysis and those of object relations theory in ways that come to constitute a major building block of Relational Psychoanalysis with its emphasis on dissociation and self-state changes that occur in the psychoanalytic field. Bromberg's influence on this new, disruptive approach to psychoanalysis that would bring together interpersonal theory, object relations theories, trauma work, multiple self state theory, and an emphasis on dissociation as a central feature of mental work, cannot be overstated. His extraordinary, personal, literary, deeply evocative clinical writing made the new relational way of theorizing and presenting clinical work vivid and accessible, making Bromberg's work central to the relational turn in psychoanalysis till his death in 2020, and beyond, as his writing remains enormously influential and his many students, patients, and supervisees continue to mine his deep contributions to clinical psychoanalysis.

Getting back to the Fall of 1988, when I learned that he would be joining the NYU Postdoctoral Program as faculty in the new Relational Track, I acted quickly, calling him right away to see if I could book what I knew would be a competitive supervision slot. At that time, in the 1980s, there were still more analytic candidates than there were supervisors with open hours (this was the late "golden age" of psychoanalysis), and so candidates felt lucky to get on long waiting lists to eventually get a spot with a "hot" supervisor, and Philip would certainly be that. Still, he seemed genuinely delighted to get my call, which he answered with a wonderfully warm voice and an enthusiastic, "Great!!, I would love to work with you!, when do you want to start?" So I became his first supervisee at NYU, and he my last supervisor—and as Rick Blaine said to Louis at the fade out in Casablanca, that was the beginning of a beautiful friendship. Philip and I were both addicted to Humphrey Bogart movies, often quoting them to one another. Casablanca was one of our favorites. He re-watched it in his last days.

Like Velleda, I recognize and was a beneficiary of the radically personal nature of the way Philip practiced, supervised, and taught; and that each of his many students, patients, and supervisees had their own Philip, not quite the same as any other. When I teach or supervise in a way that I know is closely aligned with what I learned from Philip, I recognize that I am not offering an unalloyed replica of what I learned from him—rather his influence on my way of working and thinking about the work is powerfully present for me, but in a way that is specific to my own psychic life and sensibilities. Philip once joked as we were giving a presentation together that "Tony and I often finish each others' sentences, but often in the wrong way!" That got a laugh, from me because it was true. He would often offer a perspective on what was unfolding as we discussed clinical work that seemed entirely new, utterly unpredictable, taking me by surprise, as he recognized a part of the patient or a part of me that I hadn't seen coming. And he appreciated moments in which I could return the favor, showing him a part of himself or his patient that may have gone missing as well. For many of those years, we worked together in a small group that included our close friend and trusted colleague, Anita Herron. The mutuality of such moments kept our clinical discussions alive and interesting for decades with the safe surprises that come of encountering another in intimate and challenging circumstances, committed to speaking "the truth" as each of us has access to our own at any given moment. This is as true in consulting about our work with our colleagues as it is in the psychoanalytic work that we do with our patients. As Bromberg understood, these are both, and equally, forms of psychoanalytic exploration that he, and we, loved so much.

Bromberg was always Bromberg, and he insisted that Bass be Bass, and Ceccoli be Ceccoli. His appreciation of each person's unique way of being as the heart of what we had to offer, to our patients and to each other and his appreciation of the uniqueness of each person's gifts was what made working with him always alive and surprising. Working with Philip was not without its challenges though. His insistence that every encounter meet the high and demanding standard of the "really real," meant that anything less than that would be interrogated with a lot of force and sometimes heat. He had a kind of X-ray vision, the experience of which was accentuated by the thick eyeglasses through which he peered with great intensity. The experience of this could be like the bit in Larry David's *Curb Your Enthusiasm*, in which, when Larry thought someone might not be telling the truth, he looked directly and intensely into that person's eyes, from inches away, as though to see into the person's soul to find the truth of it. Such moments can be uncomfortable for the person being scrutinized. Philip displayed his own version of that look, with a big inviting appreciative smile and twinkle in the eye when all felt free and clear, open, and "on the level." But with an intensely skeptical, interrogating look if a self behind the self was sending a message that was contradicting the intended but incomplete one. His mind was a finely tuned instrument for detecting the presence of anything false. If he came upon something in a communication that smacked of falseness, he pursued what was behind the veil as far and as forcefully as he could. I think many of us who had lifelong relationships with Philip had times with him that were quite challenging, forcing us to find more of ourselves, and more of him, than we knew were there. It wasn't always easy, but it was more than worth the trouble. In meeting Philip Bromberg in all of the diverse ways that knowing him for so many years and through so many phases of our lives entailed, I came to know more of myself (Philip would have said, "more of my selves," than I would otherwise have encountered. For that I am eternally grateful.

In the pages that follow, Velleda and I hope to offer you (our readers) our own versions of Philip Bromberg's work, as we knew it and integrated it into our own ways of working and thinking. The book represents what we distilled in our (combined) 60 years of working with Philip Bromberg over the trajectories of our own long careers, from our thirties to our sixties. His three books and numerous papers are available for you to read, and easy to find. We hope you will avail yourselves of the remarkable experience of reading his work.

This book is no substitute for that, but we hope that in offering our own views of how Philip Bromberg's work influenced our own, the valuable lessons learned in our encounter with him, it will offer another way that you might encounter one of the most creative clinical minds of our times.

Anthony Bass

About the Authors

Anthony Bass is an adjunct associate professor and clinical consultant at the NYU Postdoctoral Program, in addition to being on the faculty and a training and supervising analyst at the Columbia University Center for Psychoanalytic Training and Research. He is a founder and president of the Stephen Mitchell Relational Study Center, a founding director of IARPP, and founding editor and Editor Emeritus of *Psychoanalytic Dialogues: The International Journal of Relational Perspectives.*

Velleda C. Ceccoli, PhD, is on the faculties of the NYU Postdoctoral Program in Psychotherapy and Psychoanalysis, The Stephen Mitchell Center, and The Institute for Relational and Self Psychologies in Milan, Italy. She is also on the editorial boards of *Psychoanalytic Dialogues* and *Studies in Gender and Sexuality.* Velleda writes the ongoing psychoanalytic blog *Out of My Mind,* and has published numerous journal articles on language, trauma, dissociation, sexuality, gender, and erotic experience. She maintains a private practice in New York.

Acknowledgments

First and foremost, I want to thank my wife, partner, and first and best editor for everything I have written, Laura Geringer Bass, without whose love, support, and help I would not have been able to write this book (or anything else I have written). Another person without whom this book would have no reason to be is Philip Bromberg, whose ideas about psychoanalysis and whose personal mentorship and friendship over the years formed the basis for this book about his work. I am grateful to Velleda Ceccoli for joining me in this project and for her seamless collaboration, support, and deep understanding of Philip's work in bringing his work to life in a way that made the project possible, rewarding, and fun to work on together. I am grateful, too, to Dr. Anita Herron, with whom I met, together with Philip, weekly for a quarter of a century, discussing our work with our patients and so much more as our friendships deepened over the years of our conversation.

My other mentors in relational psychoanalysis, who included my good friends and teachers Stephen Mitchell and Emanuel Ghent also had a strong hand in the creation of this book, as they played such an integral part in helping me to become the analyst and writer that I am. Like Philip, they taught me, supervised me, and inspired me in the years that they were bringing relational psychoanalysis to light at the NYU Postdoctoral Program during my candidate years in the 1980s and beyond. I want to thank my close friends, Margaret Black, Jody Davies, and Jessica Benjamin, founders and co-directors of the Stephen Mitchell Center for

Relational Studies, a labor of love in which we have joined to work together for the last 25 years to teach new generations of relational therapists, to learn together, and grow through our collaboration. Adrienne Harris, too, has been an important collaborator over the years, in teaching relational psychoanalysis, in co-leading a discussion group together with Jody Davies and me, and in collaborating on the Board of the Sandor Ferenczi Center at the New School. In addition, our time together enjoying our many lovely dinners with Philip in the last years of his life, a chance to talk about our shared history as first generation relational analysts, also inspired this project. And of course, I am most grateful to my primary guides along the way to becoming a relational psychoanalyst—my patients, with whom I continue to grow and learn from each and every day.

Anthony Bass

* * * *

A book is the work of many, not just the person who provides the words and ideas, and I have many to thank. First and foremost, my gratitude to my patients, who over the years have taught me that theory is only helpful in so much as it helps me listen and engage with curiosity, respect, and care, and that the psychoanalytic relationship requires the courage to be real. Psychoanalysis is, as Philip Bromberg has said—*a personal relationship with professional boundaries.* Without all of you, it would just be an intellectual exercise and not the transformational process it can be.

I was fortunate enough to train at the time of *the Relational Turn* and learn from many gifted theorists and clinicians who helped to guide me and keep me curious about the process of psychoanalysis. Though many of them, like Philip, are gone, they remain steady within me—my gratitude to my supervisors—Stephen Mitchell, Christopher Bollas, and Edgar Levenson.

To Anthony Bass, my co-author, my thanks for asking me to join you in the writing of this book, and making the process of discussing ideas and our individual Bromberg's great fun.

To Rebeca Sherman for encouraging me to start the first Bromberg study group, and to Roberto Colangeli, Nancy Curcio, Lynn Egan, Barbra Locker, Elizabeth Peyton, Melanie Suchet, and Karen Wexler—thank you for always wanting more and enlivening our discussions about Philip's work.

I am indebted to my friends and colleagues Muriel Dimen, Lisa Director, Sharon Kofman, Jean Petrucelli, Debra Rothschild, and Larry Zelnick for their endless support of my work and their willingness to share their minds and hearts with me.

And finally, my love and appreciation to those I hold in my heart for walking the hard road with me—always.

Velleda C. Ceccoli

A Short Biography
Philip M. Bromberg (1931–2020)

Born in Brooklyn, New York, in 1931, Bromberg initially pursued doctoral studies in English Literature but shifted to psychology after a now infamous incident involving one of his professor's shaming him in front of his peers for writing an essay on King Lear's personality (see Bromberg, 2000; Cavitch, 2007). He credited this incident for shifting his studies to psychology, earning his bachelor's degree from New York University in 1953, a master's degree from The New School for Social Research in 1961, and a doctorate in clinical psychology from NYU in 1967. After completing his doctorate in clinical psychology at NYU in 1967, he pursued psychoanalytic studies at WAWI (1969–72) where he would later become a faculty member, supervisor, and training analyst.

Bromberg held many academic appointments, including Adjunct Clinical Professor of Psychology at the NYU Postdoctoral Program in Psychotherapy and Psychoanalysis, Clinical Assistant Professor of Psychology at Cornell University Medical College, Assistant Attending Psychologist at New York Hospital-Payne Whitney Clinic, and Faculty and supervisor at the Institute for Contemporary Psychoanalysis. He served on the editorial boards of *Psychoanalytic Dialogues* and *Psychoanalytic Inquiry* and was co-editor Emeritus of *Contemporary Psychoanalysis*. He was a founding member of the Relational Track at the NYU Postdoctoral Program in Psychoanalysis and Psychotherapy and the Stephen Mitchell Center for Relational Studies.

Bromberg's contributions to psychoanalysis and psychotherapy are many. Bromberg's most influential contribution is his emphasis on the *normal multiplicity of self-states* within every person. He argued that individuals do not possess a single, unified self but rather a shifting constellation of self-states, each with its own perspective and reality. This multiplicity is not only a response to trauma but a fundamental aspect of human experience, manifesting in daily life, dreams, and relationships. He developed a theoretical framework for understanding how these self-states interact, sometimes harmoniously and sometimes in conflict, shaping both pathology and growth.

Bromberg was instrumental in bringing the concept of dissociation—both as a process and as a mental structure—to the forefront of contemporary psychoanalytic thinking. He elucidated how early relational trauma leads to shame-based dissociative processes, impacting the capacity for relatedness and self-organization. He viewed dissociation as a basic, healthy function that enables different self-states to operate optimally, allowing for immersion in a particular reality or affect as needed. However, in the context of trauma, dissociation can become rigid, leading to fragmentation and difficulties in integrating experience.

Bromberg developed the language and theory around the existence of multiple self-states within individuals, particularly in the context of trauma and dissociation. For Bromberg, the traditional notion of the self as unitary was a "developmentally necessary illusion" and only helpful in order to maintain a sense of self continuity, but ultimately all of us move fluidly among different self-states in response to interpersonal situations. This shifting is a normal, adaptive process and not inherently pathological but rather reflective of the plural nature of human subjectivity. Bromberg introduced the metaphor of "standing in the spaces" to describe the therapeutic task of helping patients tolerate and navigate the gaps between their dissociated self-states. He believed that growth involves increasing one's capacity to "stand in the spaces" between different aspects of the self without collapsing into one or disavowing others, thus fostering greater internal communication.

Bromberg was a key figure in the development of the relational/interpersonal approach to psychoanalysis. He argued that the therapeutic relationship is inherently a two-way, intersubjective process. For him, healing occurs not through the use of technique or interpretation but through the authentic, negotiated engagement between analyst and patient. He stressed that the analyst's way of being and relating—rather than specific interventions—creates the conditions for therapeutic change. Bromberg advanced an approach that viewed the therapeutic relationship as an intersubjective, negotiated process, moving away from technique to a more flexible, relational engagement. He challenged the classical, linear model of psychoanalytic progress; instead, advocating for therapeutic change as nonlinear, with progress arising from repeated enactments and the gradual negotiation of meaning between patient and analyst.

Bromberg was widely respected as a teacher, supervisor, and mentor, known for his passionate engagement with ideas, literature, and the arts. His conceptualizations of dissociation, multiplicity, and the therapeutic relationship have profoundly shaped contemporary psychoanalytic and psychodynamic practice, influencing generations of clinicians worldwide.

Philip Bromberg passed away on May 18, 2020, at the age of 89. His work remains foundational to psychoanalysis, and his books are considered classics in the field. We hope to add to the understanding of his ideas with our contribution.

The Bromberg Tree

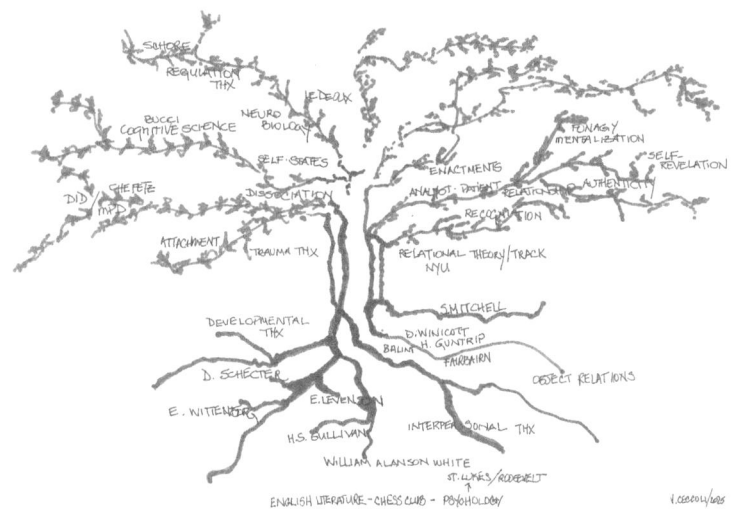

SCHORE
REGULATION THX
LEDOUX
BUCCI
COGNITIVE SCIENCE
NEURO BIOLOGY
FONAGY MENTALIZATION
SELF-STATES
SELF-REVELATION
ENACTMENTS
ANALYST-PATIENT RELATIONSHIP
AUTHENTICITY
DID / MPD
CHEFETZ
DISSOCIATION
RECOGNITION
ATTACHMENT
TRAUMA THX
RELATIONAL THEORY / TRACK NYU
DEVELOPMENTAL THX
S. MITCHELL
D. WINICOTT
BALINT
H. GUNTRIP
FAIRBAIRN
D. SCHECTER
OBJECT RELATIONS
E. WITTENBERG
E. LEVENSON
H.S. SULLIVAN
INTERPERSONAL THX
WILLIAM ALANSON WHITE
ST. LUKES / ROOSEVELT
ENGLISH LITERATURE - CHESS CLUB - PSYCHOLOGY

V. CECOCU/2015

Introduction
The Work of Philip Bromberg

We invite you to take a look at the "Bromberg Tree" and the branches which represent Philip's opus. It is a visual diagram of how his thinking developed: from his interest in English literature, his rupture with academia and his shift to Psychology and Psychoanalysis. We start at the beginning and follow the development of his thinking from his work with personality disorders, his interest in Interpersonal Sullivanian theory and developing its clinical applications, his inclusion of key concepts in British objects relations and his collaboration in creating and shaping Relational theory along with his friend and colleague Stephen Mitchell.

The book is organized into two parts. Part I consists of four chapters that follow the development of Bromberg's theoretical contributions to psychoanalytic theory. Part II looks at clinical Bromberg in action and consists of three chapters which cover his view and the development of what occurs in the analytic situation and the importance of the relationship between analyst and patient.

While we have written the book beginning with Bromberg's theoretical contributions and move to his clinical applications after we want to make sure that the reader understands that Bromberg's theories about mind, personality, relationships, and intersubjectivity are all derived from his clinical practice and not the other way around. It is perhaps the fact that Bromberg built his theories from the clinical psychoanalysis he practiced and what he observed in his relationship(s) to his patients that makes his work so sought after by clinicians.

DOI: 10.4324/9781003381853-1

Bromberg's written work begins in the late 1970s when he was still a candidate at William Alanson White and spans more than three decades. During this time he developed and applied his own theory regarding the multiplicity of the self, as well as his own brand of dissociation—singlehandedly bringing dissociative personality disorders (aka multiple personality disorders) back into psychoanalysis as lived realities. Along the way, he introduced an elegant psychoanalytic theory of trauma which had been neglected since Freud's suppression of the seduction theory.

Philip remained an Interpersonal-Relationalist (as he referred to himself) throughout his professional career, firmly planted in both camps. It was his interest in clinical psychoanalysis that led him to write, and to search for answers that expanded interpersonal theory, and in particular, Sullivan's ideas about dissociation, his representation of good me and not me states, and their clinical application to trauma. Philip often had to step out of his roots in Interpersonal theory in order to explore the why's of the clinical material he worked with. It was his engagement in working with "difficult" personalities (schizoid, narcissistic, and borderline) that led him to the British object relationists and their use of regression as necessary to successful treatment. We explore Bromberg's introduction of the concept regression into interpersonal theory and his weaving of it into Sullivan's work and his clinical application of it in Chapter 1.

Chapter 2 focuses on Philip's view of the mind as dissociative and his reconsideration of trauma, not only as a disruptive event but as an unavoidable developmental event. His elaboration of the notion of relational trauma led him to reconsider developmental theory and attachment research from a psychoanalytic lens. It also instigated his interest in trauma and his study of the field of traumatology and dissociative disorders. We then focus on Philip's development of dissociation as a normal mind-brain process, which can become a defensive mental structure in order to ensure psychic survival. In this chapter we also explore the role of perception and its influence on memory.

In Chapter 3 we engage Bromberg's concept of enactments as central to the therapeutic action, inevitable and necessary in order to establish the involvement of state sharing in their resolution. Here we also focus on the role of language, cognition, and his notion of safety versus growth.

Chapter 4 follows Bromberg's interest in cognitive science and the neurobiology of the brain and emotions and his integration of them into his clinical theory of trauma and dissociation. It highlights his collaboration with Alan Schore and Wilma Bucci, leading to the importance of affect regulation in the processing of enactments and trauma, as well as the concept of state sharing as an integral part of treatment.

Chapter 5 considers the paradox of Bromberg's clinical method and highly distinct approach to clinical praxis with his view that technique per se constitutes more of a problem for psychoanalysis than any solutions technique would purport to provide. We look at the distinction Bromberg draws between technique and method more broadly conceived, in the light of his clinical approach.

Chapter 6 focuses the central place of "Listening" as a major focus in Bromberg's way of working clinically, in teaching and in consulting. In this chapter we explore the distinct quality of Bromberg's approach to this primary psychoanalytic function at the heart of clinical work.

Chapter 7 focuses on several key areas of Bromberg's clinical contribution—Ways of Working with Dissociation, Multiplicity, Enactment, and Self-State Work in mind. We regard these dimensions of his clinical approach as at the heart of his method and unique contribution to clinical praxis.

Part I

Chapter 1

Bromberg the
Interpersonal–Relationist

Harry Stack Sullivan knew about trauma. He knew a *lot* about trauma. And he knew about it personally. Too personally. He knew a lot about dissociation, too. But he never showed how or if he worked with it clinically. As an analytic candidate, I was frustrated—and finally gave up—trying to discover where in Sullivan's writing I might find something that would help me *work clinically* with dissociation. It wasn't there. What was there was his brilliant insight into what it was and how it—dissociation—manifested itself. But nowhere to be found was anything that helped me as a clinician. I have now come to understand why. And, in the process of discovery, I came to appreciate why the secret relationship between "Dr. Sullivan," the genius, and the trauma survivor who always accompanied him—the hidden child I call "Harry"—provides a chance for me to finally offer my recognition of the extent to which his phrase "more simply human than otherwise" is an overdue tribute to their relationship and to the breathtaking conceptualization of what it means to be human, which revolutionized psychoanalytic thinking—a feat that was accomplished *through* this relationship, *because* of it, and in *spite* of it.

(Bromberg, 2014)

While training at the William Alanson White Institute, Bromberg worked with Earl Wittenberg, David Schecter, and Edgar Levenson as his supervisors. Each influential in their own way, he credited Levenson more than anyone else for the idea that the analyst is always unconsciously involved with the patient in versions of problematic relationships from the patient's earlier life, and for the

DOI: 10.4324/9781003381853-3

notion that psychoanalytic involves absorbing that unconscious influence and then making the best use of it. Levenson (1972, 1982, 1983, 1991) viewed this as part of the transformational aspect of the therapeutic action. Bromberg also attributed to Levenson the advancing of his clinical understanding of Sullivan by asserting that the analyst is not only a participant observer, but that she or he participates at an unreflective level in the transference, and that it is this dynamic participation that becomes a powerful link for therapeutic growth. For Bromberg the Interpersonalist, the focus was on the effects of his own participation as a central element in his listening stance, and analytic work involved an interaction between himself and his patient that facilitated the capacity for the analyst to understand sequestered and dissociated elements of the patient's experience through his own experience.

From the beginning of his clinical work as an interpersonal psychoanalyst, Bromberg believed that the clinical symptoms that he saw in the consulting room did not derive from intrapsychic conflict but, rather, from the kinds of destructive interpersonal events that he eventually came to refer to as developmental (and later) relational trauma. A student and devotee of Harry Stack Sullivan, Bromberg found that his own work with difficult personality disorders required more than a pragmatic/operational approach. In fact, it required him to enter the very space that Sullivan had once designated as "the mess" (Bromberg, 1998c, p. 25), referring to working with transference–countertransference dynamics, which Sullivan did not believe to be clinically useful. For Sullivan, growth involved an increasing awareness and insight of one's interpersonal relations through the analytic process of consensual validation. Thus, the curative factor of (Sullivanian) psychoanalysis emphasized the accuracy of mutually shared perceptions and minimized conditions that worked against rational inquiry. In Sullivan's self system, the self is the guardian of stability and regulates anxiety, excluding from awareness anything that would threaten its sense of security, even at the cost of personal growth. This included affective experience communicated via transference–countertransference as well as what Sullivan termed severe anxiety.

Bromberg, on the other hand, felt that there exists an area of raw experience that cannot be accessed with words and language, and needs to be experienced within the analyst–patient dyad. For him, the seeming avoidance of this mutual area of experience revealed a gap in Sullivan's clinical theory. While working within this area of experiential knowing, Bromberg found the notion of regression, as used by the British Independent group of object relations theory, to be most useful in addressing the clinical situations he was encountering. In his early papers, Bromberg set out what later became a lifetime clinical and intellectual project: filling in the gaps in Sullivan's clinical psychoanalysis through his own study of trauma, dissociation, and multiplicity and his direct engagement of these phenomena in the clinical situation. What Sullivan had termed as severe anxiety, Bromberg felt was best described as trauma.

Regression as an Interpersonal Process

Bromberg's (1979a) first psychoanalytic article, "Interpersonal psychoanalysis and regression," marked his incorporation of regression as it was understood by the British object relations writers of his time (Winnicott, Guntrip, Fairbairn, and Balint) into Interpersonal theory. It proved to be quite a debut in the psychoanalytic world. In Bromberg's way of thinking, the British Object Relations' group valued subjective experience as a "state" of mind in itself. What Sullivan had termed "the mess" was for object relations the location of the "true" self (à la Winnicott), an area of experience where meaning could not be put into language and had to be recognized through the experience of the analytic relationship. The inner world of the patient, as well as the main players in it, was to be experienced in the analytic setting. Here there was no avoidance of the transference–countertransference dynamics but rather an understanding of them as felt and lived experiential truths. For Bromberg, building this bridge between interpersonal Sullivanian theory and object relations theory added an essential and necessary component to clinical work and to interpersonal theory. Now the internal object world of the patient was observable through intersubjective relating and it was the interactional in the interpersonal that led and encouraged regression. So that, for Bromberg, regression was not brought about by prohibiting drive gratification as classical psychoanalytic theory suggests, but rather it developed as part of the process of growth, through the analyst's deep resonance with the patient's emotional experience. For him, regression is an experience that is accepted by the analyst through the nature of his attuned and receptive participation rather than one that is called for or brought about through suggestion or abstinence. For Bromberg, regression was not a concept limited to analytic work with patients having severe ego impairment, but rather a fundamental component of the psychoanalytic situation in general. In his clinical understanding, regression is an interpersonal process: one in which the analyst adapts to the patient's needs, providing the facilitative elements of parental subjectivity (Cooper, 2003). Here we already see Bromberg's interest in forging a connection between the inner and external worlds of the patient, as well as his movement toward developmental theory and parent–infant interactions.

While Bromberg's embrace of regression as an ordinary aspect of the psychoanalytic process, as well as his interest in other aspects of object relations thinking (e.g., Bromberg, 1979b, 1984, 1991) was applauded by many interpersonal readers and colleagues, including the authors of this book, he was also criticized by many others who felt that his interest in object relations theory represented a return to the intrapsychic orientation which they had been embattled with and which they had left behind. In a sense his critics were correct, as Bromberg wanted to link interpersonal psychoanalysis more firmly and thoroughly with the inner world, an emphasis that object relations had long explored. His prescient conviction—that expanding interpersonal theory toward an appreciation of primitive emotional experience opened new clinical possibilities—always remained a basic clinical tenet for him.

Emotional Development and Adaptation

Bromberg was most interested in understanding the fundamental quality of human experience and developing a theory of mind that would best account for that experience. His work with David

Schecter, in particular, led him to an appreciation of developmental theory and the role of early mother–infant experience in structuring the psyche. Such a developmental perspective enhanced his work with character disorders by providing a deeper understanding of how early relational patterns come to shape personality. The focus is now on the quality of early attachment as being of primary importance, shaping and becoming the blueprint for future interpersonal relations. This focus on early attachment patterns blended well with Bromberg's interest in object relations theory.

For example, Bromberg considered the schizoid character as shaped around the fear of loss, rather than as a characterological withdrawal from external life. For him, the schizoid personality forms attachments, but the objects of the schizoid's affection must be possessed in order to insure they will never be lost. In Bromberg's integration of object relations theory into interpersonal theory, he also shifts our understanding and definition of psychological defenses: from a reactive theory of defense (detachment) to an adaptive response that attempts to make the most of what is given in development. The movement here is from a pathological, reactive, and defensive view of intrapsychic conflict to a necessary *adaptation* to environmental, familial, and interpersonal factors. This provided a way of viewing the principal organization(s) that a person uses to adapt to other people and to life in a way that enhances his or her sense of being understood in the most basic of ways—recognized at an affective level.

For the schizoid it is the manipulation of inner reality that becomes the dominant mode of living and narrows the scope of life in the service of what Sullivan (1953) termed the "psychopathology of stability." Stability here is seen not only as a reactive defense against an intense need–fear dilemma, but as an adaptive way of maintaining the stability of the self. Thus, the mind is seen as an environment that can remain stable and relatively secure through idiosyncratic adaptations for the schizoid individual. In the shift from an internal defense mechanism to an adaptive response that is aimed at maintaining stability, we can see the seeds of Bromberg's ideas regarding stability versus change in the analytic relationship and the need to maintain a balance between them.

Due to his initial clinical concentration on character disorders, Bromberg believed that specific patterns of attachment give more meaning to these personality configurations than what the diagnostic categories could capture. For example, the relational difficulties seen in schizoid personalities such as lukewarm attachments and the experience of loneliness, or need–fear difficulties arising from possessiveness, have their origin in ways of adapting and/or surviving early experience. Here, the quality of attachment does not depend on libidinal object constancy because the attachment is to things that are rendered safe by becoming possessions of the inner world. Loneliness and emptiness are the price the person pays for avoiding full emotional involvement. In therapy, a great deal of those full emotional states such as hate, aggression, and devouring love have to emerge and come to be experienced within the analytic relationship before stability via object constancy can be achieved.

In focusing on the development of severe personality disorders, Bromberg necessarily addressed the notion of defense mechanisms. In his view of defenses as adaptational responses, one needed to take into consideration the evolution of the particular defenses prior to the full development of the ego and of the ensuing potential to hold and work with intrapsychic conflict. Consistent with both Interpersonal theory and object relations theory, he traced the origins of defenses to their sources in early development—what classical psychoanalysts had understood as pertaining to pre-oedipal phases of development. Thus, in Bromberg's view, detachment, for example, was seen as a defense that changes in structure and meaning, depending on the stage of development at which it comes about. Bromberg argued that the stage of development at which a defense comes about had a direct impact and influence on the quality and use of that defense. In other words, the defense and its function changes with each phase of development. Here again we can see Bromberg's efforts to re-think the classical notion of defense mechanisms as static and arrested at certain developmental stages, relocating them to an adaptive response which changes along with each developmental phase.

Arguing for an experience near understanding of defenses, Bromberg focused on the use of detachment based on his work with patients with schizoid, borderline, and narcissistic personality organizations. Bromberg posited that detachment as an ego defense is different than other psychological defenses because it operates directly on the external world and the real object itself: it is the real object which becomes less important, valued, or desired. Because of this, he reasoned that we must know the purpose and function of detachment at each phase of development and whether its function has changed from earlier developmental stages. Such a revision in our understanding of the mechanisms of defense shifted their psychoanalytic meaning from something one must work to break down to something one must understand the function of and move along with moment to moment, keeping close to the patients' experience of themselves. Working with defenses in this way allows us as clinicians to use them as a potential index of the patient's capacity for relatedness and his or her ability to use the analytic relationship. In order to work with such character pathology he advocated maintaining an empathic stance that can *feel* for the aspect of self that is closest to the surface of detachment. This is so that we might also feel why detachment is needed and how it serves the patient.

Bromberg capitalized on the idea that psychological development has uneven growth spurts along with periods of reorganization and stability, where there is a breaking down of established ways of being as well as periods of rebuilding. He felt that the conditions that facilitated growth involved an analytic environment that encouraged the emergence of discordant experiences while holding the self sufficiently safe so that its stability does not have to be protected at the expense of development. Such an interpersonal environment permits regression rather than inducing it. In order to grow, the self must allow itself to become less intact (to regress), so that the deeper the regression the greater the reverberation in the organization of the self.

Here again, we can see the beginning of the notion of stability versus growth, as well as the development of Bromberg's concept of the multiplicity of the self and the function(s) that each self (state) might serve relationally.

The Relational Paradigm

During the 1980s we witness the birth of the relational movement and the paradigm shift toward field theory, with a focus on the interpersonal context as shaping the development and process of the therapeutic action. The term "relational," originally coined by Greenberg and Mitchell (1983), begins to be used to delineate dyadic interactions as central to psychoanalysis, and to encompass theories identifying mind as shaped via early attachments and personality based on the interaction of early relational configurations: both intrapsychic and interpersonal. Thus Klein, Winnicott, Ferenczi, Fairbairn, Sullivan, and Kohut are all important theorists within it without carrying definitive authority. Several key ideas are born from this shift, among them the notion that early relationships create internal representations that then shape the individual's intimate relationships and personality development, as well as the notion that, if pathology is understood in terms of developmental ruptures, "untreatable" character disorders can be treated psychoanalytically.

Stephen Mitchell is at the head of this paradigm shift brought on by his ideas regarding psychoanalytic theories focusing on a two-person, dyadic model of psychoanalysis. Mitchell's interest in community psychology as well as interpersonal psychoanalysis led him to create a psychoanalytic shift that involved many great thinkers, among them Philip Bromberg, Emmanuel Ghent, Bernie Friedland, and James Fosshage. Quite literally, psychoanalytic theory was revolutionized and forever changed.

Bromberg's relationship and collaboration with Mitchell is of import here. Mitchell had been Bromberg's student at the William Alanson White Institute, where Philip taught Comparative Theories of Therapeutic Action. It was there that they began an ongoing dialogue about interpersonal theory, object relations, the illusion of oneness, Sullivan's self-system and the multiplicity of the self, as well as clinical interventions which spurred many of Bromberg's later ideas on self states, the dissociative quality of the mind, and the entwinement of the interpersonal and the intersubjective. It was Mitchell who initially spoke of the illusion of being one self as necessary and housing multiple other parts of the self. And it was also Mitchell who addressed the many difficulties and challenges encountered in childhood, along with the inevitability of parental failure and the effect of early interactions between children, parents, and the environment. While Mitchell did not use the term developmental or relational trauma, he certainly described it in his early writing (Mitchell, 1988).

The think tank that Mitchell brought together comprised the early discussions around relational theory, it included Emmanuel Ghent, Jessica Benjamin, Lewis Aron, Jody Messler Davies, Adrienne Harris, Muriel Dimen, and Neil Altman, to name a few, and provided a fertile ground for Bromberg's thinking and the development of his theory of dissociation as well as his ideas about treatment and the patient–analyst relationship. Furthermore, Bromberg credited Mitchell for encouraging him to write in journals as well as his books.

During this period of time, Bromberg published two papers (1979a, 1980a) addressing the relationship between Sullivan's interpersonal theory and object relations theory. He was attempting to bridge the two by taking Sullivan's ideas on personification (the mental representation of the self, and the self's relationships to others—good me, bad me, not me), and the idea of consensual validation—the process where the analyst as participant observer is the agent representing reality and objectivity within the interpersonal field.

For Sullivan, the analyst's therapeutic function is to connect parataxis (the mental distortions formed about relationships) to syntaxis (a more integrated view of relationships and self-participation). So that it is the maturational level of the patient's representational world that determines whether consensual validation is possible as a therapeutic process, and further, whether (and how) the therapeutic action is constituted in the relationship.

Here Bromberg began to highlight the importance of the maturational level of the patient's personifications and internal representations as crucial for the development of consensual validation and the forging of a therapeutic alliance. But most importantly, he further continued his suggestion that Sullivan's personifications had to be extended along a developmental continuum to clarify the distinctions between the self and the self-system, providing a theoretical basis for the change in mental representation(s) that comes about with change in psychoanalysis. Bromberg focuses on developmental theory (Piaget, in Bromberg, 1980a) and Sullivanian operationalism to do this, as he has already incorporated object relations theory in his thinking. It seems to us that this was a purposeful way of beginning to include attachment research and the internal world, as well as primary process, as something that enriches the analytic position and relationship into interpersonal psychoanalysis. In fact, it might have been why he embraced relational psychoanalysis with such passion and fervor. Bromberg was always interested and immersed in the internal world of his patients and searching for a way to link that with interpersonal theory.

Bromberg begins by delineating a developmental basis for Sullivan's ideas using Piaget's concepts of conservation and operational thought (Bromberg, 1980a). He then links these to Sullivan's development of mental processes as both continuous in their natural evolution and discontinuous in the way that maturity takes place, making the crucial differentiation between what we would call internal experience (as non-verbal and felt) and the external world (which becomes symbolized through an other and language learned in that relationship). Since operational thought—à la Piaget—requires another person to begin to translate and mediate what has previously been based on need satisfaction and felt experience, it is the relationship to the other that ushers in the importance of the interpersonal in validating the self-system. This parallel allows Bromberg to then speak about non-verbal experience (parataxic thinking à la Sullivan) and the need to address raw experience as the very basis of analysis and what leads to change. It is a link that leads Bromberg to begin to look at the therapeutic value of the relationship in psychoanalytic treatment and to break down the role of the analyst: both in terms of participant observation and in terms of consensual validation. Because consensual validation and much of (interpersonal) psychoanalysis relied on language, and because Bromberg believed that there are areas of experience that cannot be understood or worked with using language, but instead require the analyst to experience their patient's experience in order to know it, he begins to address the analyst's non-verbal participation (tenderness, empathy) as a way of validating the patient and making them feel known. This is the beginning of what he will later elaborate as developmental and relational trauma, providing the necessary link to attachment theory, fine tuning the analyst's participation to include the concept of authenticity and recognition.[1]

Throughout his theoretical and clinical work, Bromberg remained deeply respectful of intrapsychic life, and when he eventually formulated his views on dissociation and the multiplicity of self, he portrayed the inner world and the outer one in continuous interaction, as he found it impossible to separate them.

Note

1 Bromberg agreed with Benjamin on the idea that recognition is mutually regulating and in fact initiates the process of affect regulation. For this reason it is an essential element of the process of growth in the analytic dyad. For Bromberg the analyst's act of recognition involves a willingness to explicitly share their state of mind and put it into words for the patient. He viewed this as a necessary revelation rather than a self-disclosure.

Chapter 2

Trauma, Dissociation, and the Multiplicity of the Self

> What makes it possible, through a relationship, to link two functionally dissimilar information processing modes in the brain? My answer is a "safe enough" interpersonal environment to permit an enacted replaying and symbolization of early traumatic experience, without blindly reproducing the original outcome.
>
> (Bromberg, 2004)

During his lifetime, Philip Bromberg elegantly integrated psychoanalytic, developmental, trauma, and neurobiological data to explore dissociation as a process and as a brain structure. He believed the mind to be comprised of both dissociation and the capacity for intrapsychic conflict. He viewed trauma and psychoanalysis as inextricably linked through the concept and clinical process of dissociation, and wanted to return a usable, experience-near theory that included a multiple self-state model to psychoanalysis. This is exactly what he did. Bromberg's theory of self-states and the multiplicity of the self has had a major influence on the practice of psychoanalytic psychotherapy and trauma based therapies—introducing psychoanalysis in the treatment of trauma and returning a sophisticated theory of trauma and dissociation to psychoanalytic thinking.

Trauma

From the beginning of his clinical work, Bromberg was attentive to the non-verbal communications of his patients. This was one of

DOI: 10.4324/9781003381853-4

the reasons why he emphasized the concept of therapeutic regression used by the British Middle group of Object Relations in his brand of interpersonal psychoanalysis. He also felt that language could not access certain key experiences that had to be communicated through intense affect that was shared so that it could be felt to be known. Given Bromberg's interest in Sullivan, it was no surprise that dissociation and self-states—read me's and not-me's in Sullivanian language—became central to his thinking and clinical work. While he certainly had studied Sullivan and taught him for many years, he remained curious about Sullivan's clinical application and felt that, in remaining wedded to an operational model that dealt with what was observable and eschewed countertransference as important data, Sullivan was missing important clinical information. For Bromberg, it was the study of psychological trauma in the context of his clinical work that led the way to his thinking regarding dissociation and the multiplicity of the self, self-states, and the therapeutic value of enacted communication. Bromberg came to view these as extensions of Sullivan's theory of dissociation and necessary additions to clinical process.

Bromberg's parallel interest in Sullivanian psychoanalysis and developmental trauma allowed him to focus on non-verbal experience and early parent–child experiences as formative and constitutional. Enter David Schecter, an influential supervisor while Philip was a candidate at the William Alanson White Institute. Schecter's research in attachment and developmental theory greatly influenced Bromberg and led him to take a deep dive into the study of early trauma, not only in psychoanalysis but later within the field of traumatology. Schecter's (1973) ideas related to the infant's perception of maternal anxiety, as well as those regarding attachment, detachment, and in particular, *strangeness* anxiety, which he considered a disorder of recognition affecting the infant's present and future relations, proved to be instrumental to Bromberg's concept of multiplicity and dissociation as the result of developmental trauma and its significance in shaping the human personality.

According to Schecter, it is the maternal failure to render the strange into something novel and engageable that traumatically disrupts the infant's continuity of being. Thus, for Bromberg,

Schecter's formulation defined trauma in terms of the degree to which it cannot be held or contained by the individual without being flooded by interpersonal experience that cannot be understood and/or integrated. In Bromberg's own words: Schecter, in a powerful coup de maître, linked it to Sullivan's description of anxiety induced in the infant by the anxiety of the mothering one through a "not yet defined interpersonal process to which I apply the term empathy" (Sullivan, 1953, p. 41).

Schecter (1973, pp. 31–33) suggested that the "empathic linkage" may be mediated by the fact that "when the mother's anxious or distressed she appears as both familiar and strange to her infant," and he speculated that this seemingly unfathomable form of affect transmission described by Sullivan may be concretely "the shock of strangeness." The operative dynamism that Schecter suggested is the internalization of the feeling of badness that the child ends up with through failure of responsiveness to what is most genuine in them. Sullivan's "anxious mother" was a mother who to Schecter is behaving in a manner that communicates to the infant that the infant is not giving her pleasure; she is thus responding to her infant in a way that is going to be "strange" to the infant.

> Strangeness, to Schecter, is a phenomenon that has an impact at various levels. It is primarily an interpersonal integration, not just the perception of a quality inherent in the object (like the position of the mother's body or the shape of her mouth) when she is anxious. The "strangeness" has to do with the mother's anxiety creating a perception in the infant that is disjunctive with the infant's experience of her when she is not anxious; a total configuration of visual, kinesthetic, auditory, and interactive cues that is incompatible with the infant's self-experience as a valued participant in a relationship that feels "good."
>
> (Bromberg, 1995)

Bromberg believed that Schecter (1973) was foreshadowing the contemporary rediscovery of the significance of trauma in the shaping and reshaping of human personality. We will return to this prescient belief in the chapter where we discuss the neurobiology of attachment patterns and the formation of the self. For now, suffice it to say that it was Schecter who influenced Bromberg's views on developmental trauma and its sequelae. This constituted the beginning of what would be elaborated later as relational trauma and the link to attachment theory.

> The reason that developmental trauma (also termed relational trauma) is of such significance is that it shapes the attachment patterns that establish what is to become a stable or unstable core self. In the face of psychological trauma, self-continuity is threatened, and this threat, for most human beings, is countered by the use of dissociation as an evolutionary response that is … important to survival.
>
> (Bromberg, 1996, p. 113)

Bromberg believed that developmental trauma is inescapable and true for everyone, patients and analysts alike, regardless of attachment quality or patterns. This was an elaboration of Mitchell's belief that parental failures were inescapable. It was Bromberg's belief in the universality of relational trauma that shaped his approach to clinical practice of psychoanalysis.

Dissociation and the Multiplicity of the Self

For Bromberg, self-experience originates in relatively unlinked self-states, each coherent in its own right and composed of relational experiences that carry various meanings about the self and the self in interaction with others. The experience of being a unitary self is an acquired, developmentally adaptive illusion for all of us which can become traumatically threatened by abrupt, overwhelming input that cannot be processed through thought and language.

In traumatic situations, the mind, if able, enlists its ability for normal dissociation as a protective solution to assure self-continuity, in order to do this it suspends linkages between (previously cohesive) self-states, preventing certain aspects of self (along with their respective constellations of affects, memories, values, and cognitive capacities) from achieving access to the personality within the same state of consciousness. This is a proactive *and* protective solution to the self becoming flooded and overwhelmed by unexpected and dysregulating affect. Rather than sharing a relatively fluid state of being which allows for the processing of incoming information, the self goes on alert and shuts down internal communication (between self-states) in order to deal with affective overload and survive. Survival here (and always) is of the highest priority.

Through his own studies of traumatology and dissociative personality disorders, as well as his belief that the self is not unitary but rather comprised of many selves, Bromberg approached dissociation within a continuum or range of experience: both as a normal process *and* as a defensive structure. Dissociation as a *normal process* of the brain takes care of routine everyday living and also takes care of emergencies that could threaten self-continuity. It works as a screen for the "noise" of life situations as well as an immediate responder to crises in everyday life. However, in the aftermath of trauma, dissociation is enlisted within a mental structure that becomes pathological because its highest priority is to keep self-states from freely communicating with each other so that survival is insured. This pathological structure requires an eternal vigilance that robs the self of the ability to move fluidly between one's self-states and live life creatively, spontaneously, and with pleasure. This is the dissociative structure that as analysts we are relating to during enactments with patients.

So, as a *defense* against trauma, dissociation serves to protect the mind from being overwhelmed by more than it can process *in the present moment*, providing "the escape when there is no escape" (Putnam, 1988, p. 104) from trauma in real life whether it is massive or developmental. As a *protection*, the process of dissociation is enlisted into the creation of what becomes a mental structure in its own right—a structure that is used by the brain as an automatic "smoke detector" (Schore, in Bromberg, 2011) to proactively protect the mind/brain against any possible return of dysregulated and/or potentially disorganizing affective experience that has been sequestered and remains cognitively unsymbolized.

Dissociation as a defense functions to protect the stability of self by controlling traumatic affect that cannot be regulated. It differs from repression in that it alienates the patient from aspects of the self that are inconsistent and felt to be unbearable with their experience of who they are, whereas repression avoids mental content that may lead to unpleasant intrapsychic conflict. With dissociation one is unable to see themselves through the eyes of the other, lacking the ability for intersubjectivity and making interpersonal negotiation difficult, if not impossible. Repression as a defense is responsive to anxiety, dissociation as a defense is responsive to trauma.

The essence of dissociation, according to Bromberg, is that it alters perceptual experience, draining the interpersonal context of personal meaning by unlinking the mind from its reflective perception of dyadic affective experience, thus effectively isolating the person from the "danger" of experiencing the other's otherness. By narrowing the range of our perception, dissociation sets up nonconflictual categories of self experience as different parts of the self, or different self-states.

The mind employs dissociation both as a mental process (a defense against destabilizing affective flooding it cannot regulate or escape) and as a mental structure (a proactive "early warning system" against the recurrence of an experience that exists mainly as an affective memory held by the body) that the mind is never quite sure what really happened in the first place (Bromberg, 2011). This explains why memory for the traumatic event can often be spotty, minimal, or faulty, since the trauma lives in affective memory which is not organized in time, nor by language or cognition. Or as Bromberg puts it, "in the interest of preserving ego stability, discrete, affectively intense events that are inconsistent with narrative memory are largely deprived of a self-context into which they can be accessed and cognitively processed" (Bromberg, 1998a, p. 185).

What keeps unsymbolized experience so rigidly unyielding to cognitive understanding and reflection is that it is organized around elements more powerful than the factual evidence of reason or cognition can apprehend—what has been termed *implicit relational knowing*[1]—a relational process of communication that is experience based. Thus, the more intense the anxiety of triggering unprocessed traumatic affect, the more powerful the dissociative forces, and the harder it is for episodic or working memory to cognitively represent the here-and-now event that is triggering the affect, or to access long-term memories associated with it. In fact, the message is a sub-symbolic one that speaks through affect (Bucci, 2003). This is why words and verbal language may not be able to access or help process the event or trauma, and in fact may re-traumatize the patient. When we look at the neurobiology of emotions and the brain we will elaborate on the structural reasons why language is often ineffective when working with trauma.

Let us go back to developmental and attachment theories, this time with a focus on language. Before the onset of speech, communication takes place through parent–child affectively regulated patterns of relational interchange in which familiar, repetitive patterns of interpersonal experience become known and remembered through what has come to be called procedural memory. These early interpersonal modes of relating form the child's affective core of personal identity: a highly concrete, attachment-based foundation of self-experience on which more flexible self-development will be built. Furthermore, symbolic language takes time to develop and involves the meaning acquired through parental dyadic interaction: gestures, rhythms, tones, gaze, etc. Thus, words become carriers of personal feeling based on dyadic affective communication. They require the parent's reciprocal affective aliveness as well as parental recognition of the child's interactions; when this is not available, relational ruptures occur which are the origin of relational trauma and early self-states (me's and not-me's). In Bromberg's words:

> Language alone is insufficient to mediate developmental growth. New experience of self in relation to reality is organized not by ideas but by personal imagery. There must therefore be a communication with the outside that is at the affective level of the experience for linguistic content to become integrated pleasurably.
>
> (Bromberg, 1991, p. 8)

As part of the process of being socialized through language, and for the relational construction of self-representation to take place securely, the child must be validated as who they are in the moment and through their transitions between their self-states. If this fails to happen, then words are felt as untrustworthy and empty and are not usable as affective signifiers. However, *subsymbolic* affective communication continues to participate in meaning construction throughout life; this is why we best understand what someone means by what they are "saying" when we are affectively engaged while they are saying it. And further, it turns out that what is important is not the words that are used necessarily, but *the way that they are spoken*. The prosody of our voice carries intention, authenticity, and meaning through its rhythm, intonation and affective resonance (Ceccoli, 2012).

This also brings up Bromberg's notion of authenticity and affective honesty, which for him is rarely if ever communicated through content or language per se. Rather it is communicated through a relational bond of human relatedness that also operates at the neurobiological level in what Schore has termed right brain to right brain state sharing (Schore 2003a, 2003b, 2007). Another way of thinking about intersubjectivity is through Bromberg's notion of recognition, which is about knowing and experiencing the other, as well as being able to hold the other in mind—what Fonagy et al. (2005) refer to as the ability to mentalize and D. N. Stern et al. (1998) calls relational knowing. Bromberg was appreciative of Fonagy's mentalization theory, viewing it as a valuable developmental framework that complemented his own work on dissociation and self-states. He recognized mentalization as a crucial developmental process that can be compromised by trauma and dissociation, and viewed the capacity to mentalize as something that becomes "frozen" or impaired when dissociative processes dominate psychological functioning. He positioned mentalization as an essential developmental achievement that becomes accessible through the integration of dissociated self-states, viewing the restoration of the capacity to mentalize as a natural outcome of successful therapeutic work with dissociated aspects of the self. Bromberg conceptualized mentalization within the context of his self-state theory, suggesting that the capacity to mentalize depends on the integration and communication between different self-states. He argued that when dissociation holds "intersubjectivity captive," a person's ability to engage in the imaginative process of understanding mental states—both their own and others'—becomes severely compromised. He viewed mentalization as intrinsically linked to intersubjective processes and the capacity for self-reflection across different self-states. Bromberg emphasized that dissociation impairs intersubjectivity such that the self is "largely unable to see himself through the eyes of an other" (Bromberg, 2011, p. 50). Unlike repression that disavows the content which causes conflict, dissociation disavows parts of the self, and it is this impairment that directly affects the capacity for mentalization, which requires the ability to imagine and understand mental states.

Bromberg viewed mental functioning as an ongoing dialectic between the mind's ability to both hold conflict and dissociate. Here the issue of state-dependent memory is illustrative: when dissociation is present, memory is organized by the way something is known or experienced. He states:

> In order for unprocessed subjective experience to become symbolized in conscious awareness a link must be made between the mental representation of the event and a mental representation of the self as the agent or experiencer, these episodic representations … reside in short term or working memory.
>
> (Kihlstrom (1987) in LeDoux (1989), cited in Bromberg, 2011, p. 79)

Since trauma affects both mental content and structure, when things matter too much memory is state dependent; the more intense the (unsymbolized) affect is, the more powerful the dissociative forces that prevent linking and the more difficult it is for episodic/working memory to represent perception and access long-term memory. Furthermore, traumatic experience bypasses the hippocampus and is stored either visually or somatically, therefore returning in the form of flashbacks or physical symptoms without any cognitive meaning. This has power clinical implications as high levels of affect and/or arousal in therapy prevent cognitive processing and linking, overloading working memory and flooding the emotional centers of the brain (keeping affective and somatic experience unintegrated). Thus, the therapeutic relationship must support an internal structure that helps regulate hyperarousal in order to safely experience one's self structure as stable enough to withstand the analyst's subjectivity without the threat of being flooded by shame or panic of trauma.

Bromberg was concerned with how to understand the mental processes underlying the transition from dissociation to the capacity to hold conflict. He felt that to the degree that the capacity for internal conflict developed in areas where it had previously been foreclosed or limited, the dissociated parts of the self had to find an interface with the mind's ability to utilize (analytic) interpretation. He viewed enactments as that interface and the necessary negotiation between patient and analyst as fostering the capacity for conflict through the development of intersubjectivity. This "structural shift" from dissociation to conflict was clinically seen as an increasing capacity for a self-reflective posture in which one is able to observe aspects of the self that were previously dissociated and are now distasteful.

Note

1 Term introduced by the Boston Change Group (1998) referring to intersubjective communication that is non-verbal but known and felt.

Chapter 3

Enactments and State Sharing

> I think it is safe to assume they (enactments) begin at whatever point the part of the patient's self we are speaking about begins to feel ignored relationally because we are not affectively alive enough to it.
>
> (Chefetz & Bromberg, 2004)

Bromberg thought of enactments as the most powerful wellspring of potential for psychoanalysis as a therapeutic tool. As shared, dissociative events, enactments actually give voice to conflicting states of mind, allowing them a chance to be known within the therapeutic relationship. This "voice" is usually emotional and affect laden, involving both the analyst and the patient in a conversation that requires being experienced and felt first and decoded after. This requires the complete involvement of the analyst, and often includes their experience of shame at having become dysregulated themselves and involved with their own and with the patient's unacknowledged self-states (not-me's). It is important to note that such dysregulation does not mean that the analyst is justified in acting out but rather that the analyst, like the patient, may and probably will experience intense affect and may feel at a loss and unable to access their "professional" demeanor. For him, enactments are "an attempt to force the analyst to repair the irreparable" (Bromberg, 2006a, p. 94). And indeed, none of us can repair a past that is frozen in the lived experience of trauma. The beauty of Bromberg's clinical method is his belief that enactments demonstrate the patient's determination to be recognized and known by us as analysts, so that through that relationship the *present* can be reparative.

DOI: 10.4324/9781003381853-5

Bromberg seemed to have an exquisite sensitivity for sensing the self-states at play in the patient–analyst interaction. He felt that most clinicians can recognize the experience of their professional manner loosening as their own unacknowledged self-states are being contacted by the patients' self-states. He tells us that this is a communication that is affective and often times emotionally dys-regulating, where language and words, particularly those of the therapist might make things worse for the patient, re-enacting a familial narrative and/or the trauma of non- recognition. Because enactments are attempts to signify affective needs that are seeking expression and recognition, they often transcend the everyday behavior of the patient in their life. As such they require symboli-zation within a relationship that "hears" the affective commu-nication and makes it known in order to be metabolized, thought about, spoken, which eventually leads to emotional processing with another and growth. It is the fact that, once processed, enactments can be co-narrated within a new relational context that provides personal meaning and the opportunity for growth.

For Bromberg, words themselves are not what accounts for symbolization; rather, it is the new perceptual context that the words come to represent within the relationship to the other. He purports that words do not exist in time and space; rather, it is the meaning of the person speaking that exists and this is constructed from a perception of the words framed by the immediate context in which they are spoken (Bromberg, 2006a, p. 11). For him, the process of perceptual transition to the linguistic symbolization of experience often includes shifts in the perception of events that are efforts to begin to provide meaning to experience through a lin-guistic narrative. Thus, moving from dissociation to the ability to hold conflict first involves attending to lived experience as repre-sented schematically through perception and only later through language and a language that provides meaning through the intersubjective negotiation involved in relationships.

Bromberg felt that enactments began when as analysts we are not affectively alive enough to respond to a part of the patient that is trying to communicate with us beyond the spoken words through a feeling or emotion. This can manifest in a therapeutic attempt to interpret, or address the emotion with our "analytic" understanding. The (not-me) self-states involved in enacted communication appear as *subsymbolic* affective experiences that are received in the same manner by the therapist, "who sooner or later notices something peculiar going on—most often in himself" (Bromberg, 1998c). In other words, enacted communication requires recognition by another mind that is affectively attuned to it and affectively engaged with it. It is this affective *link* that releases the self-state which has been trapped in lived experience and the affective exchange with the analyst has the potential to begin to raise the patient's experience to the level of thought, so that it can be spoken about. So, first it has to be felt by both participants so that it can be thought about, shared, and then co-narrated. In this way of thinking, enactments are attempts at the joint meaning construction of trauma.

For Bromberg, enactments offered opportunities to re-experience the old and work through a different outcome that helps in the symbolization of the original trauma. His view is that the relational process offers the container for the patient to re-experience destabilizing affect within a different context. This is not necessarily about the therapeutic setting providing safety (although it does), but more about being able to work at the very edge of the patient's tolerance, so that affect can be experienced within the therapeutic dyad, and then cognized and symbolized. Safety within this context has implicit as well as explicit meanings. Since the therapeutic relationship is shaped as a collaboration, it is always changing, and therefore it is impossible to fully know what will feel safe to the patient and what may not. Yet, surprises for him are what provides the greatest leverage for therapeutic action (Bromberg, 2006a, p. 87). While he views them as holding the potential for creativity, spontaneity, and as the wellspring of the unconscious, he also sees them as the source of the greatest potential difficulty between analyst and patient, precisely because surprises can cross the threshold into severe anxiety and shock, becoming the harbingers of potential trauma (Bromberg, 2006a, p. 87). He further states that it is this threat that leads to the messiness of enactments and potential ruptures in the treatment. The degree to which such enactments become repetitive and unworkable between therapist and patient often speaks to a history of severe trauma, in which the unrelenting repetition of certain enactment is likely to be felt by therapist and patient alike as closer to hopelessness and despair regarding the possibility of repair and growth.

For Bromberg, safe surprises are another matter entirely. Here the patient and analyst find themselves in an area that was previously not available to either because of the intensity of the affect within it, yet it becomes available precisely because of the recognition established within the therapeutic alliance. Because safety and growth are part of the ongoing negotiation of the analytic relationship itself, and its basic principle involves what a given patient and analyst do in an unanticipated way that is "*safe but not too safe*," Bromberg advocated an analytic approach that works at the interface of stability and change, through a replaying of the relational failures of a patient's past as safe surprises. Here, safety is intended to address keeping affect dysregulation below the level that makes surprise turn to shock and destabilization. Once the patient surpasses this level of dysregulation it is impossible to think let alone symbolize traumatic experience. Thus, within an enactment, safety becomes possible because of the analyst's ability to think about what is going on, and then share it, involving the patient in a dialogue about what happened between them. This is never a clear-cut process; in fact, quite the opposite. It involves what Bromberg aptly referred to as "stumbling along and hanging in" (Bromberg, 2012b), describing a period of time during which, as analysts, we are likely to lose our bearing and knowledge, and perhaps our ability to make sense of what is happening in the room.

Part of Bromberg's ongoing interest was to highlight how interaction related to change must always involve the analyst's appreciation of the need to preserve self-stability in the attempt to reconfigure experience. For him, the source of therapeutic action is in the therapist's ability to relate fully to whatever aspect of self the patient is experiencing and presenting as "real," while not forgetting to let the other, more dissociated parts know he is aware that they too exist and are listening. For Bromberg, safe surprises and state sharing are part and parcel of the therapeutic action and process. Collisions and the negotiation of those collisions are central to his process of relational repair, and follow his belief that it is the accumulation of successful reparations that are negotiated within the analytic dyad that enables patients to grow and heal.

Multiplicity and State Sharing

Bromberg recognized the mind as operating within a self-state structure that drives the dyadic process of enactment and its ability to allow the dissociated parts of the self to be contacted within the interpersonal field. Originally, Bromberg viewed this as connecting to the patient's "raw" state of mind, but in his later work he saw it as the co-creation of a relational unconscious, a state of mind that draws on enactment and symbolic communication and belongs to neither subject while belonging to each (Bromberg, 2011, p. 154). His interest in multiplicity and self-states began with his interest in Sullivan's work and ideas regarding the self system and then moved him toward studying dissociative disorders, beginning a collaboration with Richard Chefetz with whom he shared an intellectual and clinical dialogue regarding dissociation, trauma, and the clinical process (see "Talking with me and not-me," Chefetz & Bromberg, 2004). Both advocated an experience near language that respected a multiple self-state model, attempting to bridge traumatology and psychoanalysis.

Bromberg viewed the enacted communication between patient and analyst as involving the sharing of self-states, which can only come about through relationship as it becomes safe enough for both participants to share their states of mind, even, and perhaps more so, those states of mind that are tentative and covered with shame. This is often initiated by the analyst as a form of self-revelation that is communicated in an authentic manner, which is recognized as such by the patient. Here, authenticity, the feeling that one has the patient's interests at heart, leads the way in what self-revelation (versus disclosure) is communicated. The difference between self-revelation and self-disclosure is important to note here. Bromberg considered it a revelation precisely because he was addressing his own self-states when speaking to a patient within an enactment; thus he was revealing a part of himself rather than disclosing an event or memory of his life. Bromberg stressed that such communications were an inevitable part of treatment and essential to the therapeutic process and personality growth. For him, state sharing highlighted the capacity to co-create a connection between self and other. His notion of multiplicity supported this idea since it is possible to maintain various self-states while co-creating others, in the same vein as it is possible to change while remaining the same. For Philip, these were parallel ideas.

Bromberg considered mental states to be shared space, and as always involving self–other negotiations. This is particularly true of enactments, where state sharing involves the sharing of self-states known and unknown. He believed in the *"Bromberg Common Property Principle,"* where he considered his feelings about patients not to be his personal property because he viewed them as part of an unsymbolized context within which both he and the patient held pieces that are linked sub-symbolically and not yet in language.

The dissociative process allows the sharing of mental states that are private, not necessarily known to others or to other parts of the self, and are usually awash with shame. The ability to share these turns the patient–analyst relationship into what therapy is all about. Or, put differently, for Bromberg, psychoanalysis is functioning as psychotherapy when it is facilitating the negotiating of otherness. Furthermore, he believed that there is a difference between a cure and healing: in that no one can be cured of who they are, yet a dissociative structure can be surrendered little by little because it diminishes in its value to the person (Bromberg, 2011). This is because dissociation becomes less necessary as a defensive structure for survival and becomes more usable as an assembly of working self-states. For Bromberg the surrender of a dissociative structure can only take place relationally, over time, and following an inherent interpersonal neurobiology, in that it either takes place in both partners or not at all (Bromberg, 2012b). Indeed, Bromberg held that the processes that constitute the deepest forms of interaction between analyst and patient occur through engagement with the sequestered and dissociated parts of both patient and analyst. It is precisely these collisions and negotiations that constitute the work and potential transformation of psychoanalytic treatment.

Intersubjectivity

The question of how to facilitate the cognitive symbolization of unprocessed affective experience is central to the notion of inter-subjectivity. Such affective experience has been conceptualized differently by various authors, all of whom were Bromberg's colleagues. So Bucci (1197a, 2003, 2007a, 2007b, 2010) as we have seen, refers to it as sub-symbolic, whereas Stern (1997, 2009) speaks of it as unformulated, and the idea that much of experience remains unarticulated and only becomes formulated through relational dialogue and meaning-making. Stern addresses the hermeneutic process—how meaning is made and unmade in the analytic field, and how experience takes form in language and relationship. While focusing on different areas of dissociated experience, both Stern and Bromberg prioritize relationality, dissociation, and enactment, viewing the analytic relationship as a dynamic field where unconscious experience emerges and is transformed.

A synchronous view of Bromberg's was put forth by Jessica Benjamin, whose concept of thirdness emphasizes that human relatedness requires a capacity for intersubjective communication in order to move beyond polarization of self and other. She developed the notion of a transitional mental space, a third, where recognition of the other's subjectivity becomes possible through negotiation. She further argued (Benjamin, 2007) that it is the internal wholeness experienced via recognition that supports a shared reality and a space of thirdness within which self–other negotiation(s) can take place. While Bromberg's notion of recognition is rooted in his theory of dissociation and multiplicity, he agreed with Benjamin and considered the development of inter-subjectivity in areas of the mind that were captive in a dissociative mental structure to be the basis of the therapeutic action in all forms of psychodynamic psychotherapy.

Chapter 4

The Neurobiology of the Self

Affect, Cognition, and Perception

> I've argued that being fully oneself is a capacity that requires self-state coherence to be preserved without losing awareness of the differences between the separate self-states. When this is too much for the mind/brain to handle, self-state coherence is unable to be preserved.
>
> (Bromberg, 2012a, p. 273)

Philip believed in the power of affect and that the recapturing of affect opened the door to early memories of real, and often traumatic experience (initially thought of as developmental trauma and later as relational trauma). In fact, he came to think that everyone suffered from developmental trauma of some sort, and that, despite this, the dissociative nature of the mind helped most of us work with our self-states relatively smoothly. He believed that this particular form of trauma was most relevant for psychoanalysis and psychotherapy because it shapes the attachment patterns that establish what is to become a stable or unstable sense of self. His work became about delving into the process of dissociation, allowing affect that was lost to consciousness (often unsymbolized but known through feeling) to come into being through the analytic relationship, and ultimately actualizing the links between different states of self. He was concerned with how to transform what he viewed as adaptive difficulties and survival strategies into accessible, known, and understood parts of the self. While he disliked the term integration, Bromberg worked toward making self-states known to his patients so that they could be recognized and addressed relationally, a

DOI: 10.4324/9781003381853-6

collaboration that could lead to understanding them and freeing the self toward a less restricted way of being. For him, this entailed working through enacted communication so that it could be experienced and thought of jointly.

Bromberg's interest in attachment patterns and developmental trauma led him to numerous collaborations with traumatologists, cognitive researchers, and neuro-biologists. Over time, he began to integrate these disciplines into his psychoanalytic theory of trauma and its clinical relevance and application. During my work with him (VC), we often joked that Freud would have felt avenged, given the body of neurobiological work that has validated the way that trauma impacts brain structure and behavior. Of course, Philip would note, Freud would have to reinstate the seduction theory, just like Ferenczi had implored him to. All funny business aside, Bromberg's final contributions involved his collaboration with a number of scientists and researchers, among them: LeDoux, Bucci, Galese, Putnam, and Schore, et al., interested in the psychoanalytic process as a therapeutic tool and its intersection with neurobiology.

Bromberg often used stories to introduce his ideas in his written work, and one of my favorites is about Adolf the cat, which he used when first introducing his interest in the neurobiology of the brain, affect regulation, the hard wiring of flight or fight and dissociation as a last resort response in the face of danger. Here it is in his own words:

> When I was a kid, an endless source of fascination was looking out of my bedroom window at our backyard garden to silently observe the mysterious interactions between the animals, birds, trees, bushes, and flowers. But like the Garden of Eden, it received periodic visits from an infamous inhabitant of our neighborhood: a cat, who was referred to by everyone in the vicinity as Adolf (I was a World War II kid). Adolf was an aggressive, predatory, seemingly fearless animal, whose viciousness and mean-temperedness terrorized the other neighborhood cats as well as most of the dogs. I hated this animal totally and, I think, was somewhat afraid of him myself. Adolf would suddenly appear in our garden as if by

magic—by magic, because it was a very well fenced-in area and we were never able to discover how he entered. What he seemed to enjoy most was climbing our fruit trees to see whether he could find a nest containing a baby bird or two to feast on. He seemed totally indifferent to the parent birds wildly flapping their wings and shrieking hysterically overhead (*way* overhead, I might add). In the animal world, he was sort of like the neighborhood bully.

One morning, as I was watching the action in the garden, I spotted Adolf. He was climbing stealthily up the trunk of an apple tree, clearly on his way to a nest. As he neared the top branches, two adult birds materialized, seemingly out of nowhere, and began to put on a performance that was nothing short of awesome. They were blue jays, and those birds gave new meaning to the word *tough*. Screaming, they swooped down on Adolf, reversing course inches from his head, precisely at the point beyond which Adolf's claws could not reach. I hadn't seen blue jays in our garden before this moment, nor had I ever seen them in action anywhere else, and, I suspect, neither had Adolf. Adolf and I were both in a state of shock, but for Adolf the shock was horrifyingly personal. Over and over the two jays repeated their dive-bombing until Adolf did what I had never before seen him do or believed he ever could do. He shinnied backward down the tree trunk, falling the final 8 to 10 feet, and began to run. But there was no escape. The two birds pursued him wherever he went, though he was now far from their nest. Neither the ferocity nor the precision of their aerial attacks showed any sign of diminishing, and their abrasive bird-curses became, if anything, even louder. To this day I can recognize a blue jay's call the instant I hear it, and I still love it. The sound has always reminded me of the strangely comforting rasp of a rusty clothesline pulley as the line was being yanked on by my mother. These guys were literally driving Adolf crazy, and I was cheering them on. He could not fight (because they were not reachable); he could not flee (because it was a fenced-in garden, and Adolf apparently had forgotten where his secret passageway was); and he could not hide (because they could find him wherever he was). It was then that I observed (though I didn't know it then) what I now realize was a remarkable example of dissociation as a defense against trauma—what Putnam (1992) has called "the escape when there is no escape" (p. 104). Adolf suddenly lay down right where he was and remained motionless. His body took on a strange, almost flaccid shape, and I began to wonder whether he had died of fright. The blue jays kept up their counterattack for a short while longer and then flew off. As I said, I hated this animal, and I was in no rush to help him if he was still alive. But I stayed at the window, probably somewhat numbed myself at seeing this feline terrorist reduced to mush. Was he dead?

No! Adolf, as if hit by an electric charge, suddenly sprang upright, fur standing on end, and took off to a far corner of the garden where he lay, shaking, behind a bush. As I look back on this now, I wonder what he was like after that incident. I have no recollection of him in the garden after that time, but I don't really know if that may be more of a wish than a reality. Did he develop a cat version of posttraumatic stress disorder? Maybe his memory loss for the location of his hidden tunnel was the first sign. I was probably too young to hope he was plagued by flashbacks of blue jays, but that is neither here nor there. The point of this vignette is to make as vivid as I can the power of dissociation when used as a defense. It is a defense unlike any other defense. In human beings, it bypasses cognitive modulating systems and, as LeDoux's (1989, 1994, 1996) research powerfully demonstrates, is clearly anchored in an evolutionary response that is equivalent in survival priority to certain genetically coded response patterns of lower animals to a life-threatening attack by a predator.

(Bromberg, 2001)

Indeed, over the past 25 years, research in a variety of disciplines has come to support what takes place in the mind (psychically) and between people (interpersonally). Attachment and developmental data, trauma studies, cognitive science, and neurobiological research have now converged to offer us a detailed picture of how the brain and central nervous system develop and are dependent on early caregiving and the quality of that caregiving (for a review of many of these see Schore, 1994). Furthermore, this research has established that early attachment patterns determine the quality and configuration of our relationships in later life.[1] Philip believed that our relationships as adults were imbued with relational trauma having to do with the non-recognition of parts of the self that continued to exist as not-me's within the personality structure. And further, that those self-states came alive affectively in the hopes of being finally recognized and known. Psychoanalysis provided one means of relational symbolization and growth.

Bromberg's interest in finding a clinically useful model that respected the impact of trauma (be it relational or situational) on the psyche and the way that people lived their life led him to investigate the neurobiology of the brain and human emotions. This provided the final theoretical piece to his theory of dissociation and trauma and also led him to work with affect regulation.

The Mind and the Brain

Bromberg believed the mind to be dissociative and also capable of repression as delineated in the classical conflict model. These two structural templates represented different mental and emotional systems for him. He thought that there could exist parallel, but functionally dissimilar, information processing modes in the brain each with distinct implications for understanding the complexity of subjective self-experience. Enter Joseph LeDoux (2002), who in neurobiological terms, suggests that the mystery underlying multiple selfhood reflects a parallel situation when looking at underlying brain processes and structures. In fact, LeDoux's research can be understood to show that different self-states are reliant on different brain systems which can be in sync but often are not, and it is this that can account for multiple aspects of the self to coexist.

The brain processes information via two different systems: the first, mediated by the brainstem and the limbic system, primarily the amygdala and hippocampus respectively, is responsible for the nonverbal encoding of emotion, memory, and motivation; the second, mediated primarily by the neocortex, is in charge of verbal and representational symbolization of experience. For

Bromberg, how to get the two systems to collaborate when they don't want to is the neuroscience version of the clinical question: How do clinicians talk with "me's and not-me's" so as to enable them to increasingly talk with each other as an internal process? The potential answer leads Philip back to his interest in emotions, since affect is a key player in the way information is processed.

Because the cortical symbolization of experience is divided between a sensory-based right-brain function, and a linguistically based left-brain function, right-brain encoding tends to function with pre-emptive power when the person is in an emotionally overwhelmed state, activating the brain's "fear system" (LeDoux, 1996). In order for non-verbal emotional states to be verbally represented and cognized they have to travel through the limbic system to the neocortex, a journey that is not possible in states of hyper or hypo arousal. This accounts for the failure of words and interpretive work when working with the heightened or deadened affective states that are present in trauma.

Specific brain structures within the limbic system are involved in assessing the emotional significance of incoming information (amygdala), regulating autonomic and hormonal systems and transmitting information (brainstem), and integrating incoming information with existing information and with cortical input through the hippocampus. Under conditions of emotional stability (which require balanced amygdala arousal), events are transformed into thinkable units by the hippocampus and linked into similar cognitive schemas. This increases cortical symbolization, and traumatic situations can be distinguished perceptually from others that might contain similarities but are relatively benign. In other words, symbolization of affective experience can only take place where affect is relatively stable and regulated. When emotional life is calmer, the hippocampus is better able to get the information it needs from the amygdala and to associate it to a storehouse of knowledge in the left frontal lobes and other neocortical locations, while assisting in the creation of a verbal narrative.

LeDoux's neurobiological research is consistent with Bucci's (1997b, 2011) cognitive research on the therapeutic value of enacted communication in the psychoanalytic process. She views this dimension of human communication as a sub-symbolic process for the transmission of meaning, which operates in all of our sensory modalities and is dominant in emotional information processing. In her system, these sub-symbolic representations are systematic, lawful, and organized into *emotion schemas*, which are comprised of relational memory structures that are suffused and steeped in affective experience. Her work validates the necessity of working within an area of affective tolerance, so that traumatic experiences can be re-worked therapeutically and symbolized.

Alan Schore's (2003, 2007) work has shifted attention to neuroscientific data, establishing the idea that selfhood is relational at the brain and body level, with each level having a connection to the mind level. Bi-hemispheric brain interaction varies in terms of what is tolerable, so that there exists a simultaneous maintenance of self-states while we are co-creating others.

Schore's research (1994, 2003a, 2003b) on affect regulation, trauma, and psychoanalytic treatment has advanced our knowledge of the brain structures involved in effective psychoanalytic treatment. He notes that:

> right brain attachment mechanisms are expressed within the regulating and dysregulating emotional communications of any dyad, including transference-countertransference interactions that lie at the core of the therapeutic alliance. Any successful treatment must optimally access not "the trauma" but the immature biological systems that inefficiently regulate stress, especially the right brain survival mechanism, dissociation, that is characterologically accessed to cope with dysregulating affective states.
>
> (Schore, in Bromberg, 2011, p. x)

Bromberg's work interweaves with Schore's research. In fact, his collaboration with Schore advanced many of his ideas about treatment, including how to work with enactments and affect, the role of procedural memory, the importance of non-verbal registers in maintaining affect regulation and establishing affect tolerance and the role of dissociation. According to Schore (2003a, 2003b), affect regulation rests on the use of an operative dialectic between the ability for auto regulation and relational regulation. Mature affect regulation depends on the balance in this dialectic. The focus here is on the degree to which early relational bonds are internalized as stable and secure, which will determine significant aspects of the brain's structure, especially in the right hemisphere. This will determine whether the adult is able to use interactive regulation, including a therapeutic relationship when his or her auto regulatory mechanism fails. Here, the analyst has a dual role as psycho-biological regulator and co-participant, according to Schore, and this is vital during periods of affective intensity. Bromberg believes that this supports his view that a process of collision and negotiation is therapeutic because it allows encounters with otherness.[2]

From the standpoint of dissociation, Bromberg views states of affective arousal as stemming from unprocessed developmental trauma that is mentally unbearable and therefore unavailable to thought and cognition. "In these instances of attachment related developmental trauma," Bromberg states, "the brain's fear system is activated, triggering a defensive dissociative response that insures survival. Because the preservation of self-continuity has the highest evolutionary priority, it bypasses thought to insure it" (Bromberg, 2011).

Trauma and dissociation compromise various mental functions, foremost among them is perception, because it thwarts the cognitive ability to play with images, which interferes with the use of perception in the construction of meaning. Bromberg viewed perception as a relational process—one involving a personal interaction between the mind of the individual and the external world. Therefore, what he called the "dissociative anaesthesia" of the personal interactive context that perception relies on leaves one with a sensory image of the thing itself without the necessary felt interaction needed to turn sensory experience into perception that can be thought of, played with, and used to construct personal meaning and become part of narrative memory. The individual is thus left with sort of knowing or snapshots of something but can't really say that it happened. In analytic treatment, the power of self truths must be challenged by perception according to Bromberg, which is why he views enactments as holding enormous potential for transformation and personal growth.

Bromberg views self-state organization as linked to the brain's organization of neuronal networks, so that particular emotions and feelings will not only activate particular self-states, they will also activate particular neuronal pathways in the brain. Here, Bromberg offers us what is perhaps the first neuro-biological link between the structure of the mind and the structure of the brain through his use of Edelman's (1989) theory of *neural Darwinism*. Briefly, it addresses the neurobiology of the brain as a pattern of constancy (survival through stability) and variation (growth through change), which leads to highly individualized neuronal networks. Bromberg suggests that the constancy/variation principle of the structure of the brain also presents an accurate description of the self-state structure of the mind. Thus, while part of the brain's adaptation depends on learning new information, stability has an evolutionary priority over growth.

For Bromberg, the mind's struggle between constancy and variation follows the same evolutionary priority. Thus, dissociation ensues in order to maintain self-stability and protect the mind from struggling with an emotionally threatening situation (trauma) that is inaccessible to thought. Moreover, *neural Darwinism* readjusts the brain's evolutionary function before the struggle to think becomes a source of *dys*regulation and potential depersonalization, tipping the balance between constancy and variation in favor of constancy, so that survival is insured. In other words, trauma compromises both the neuroplasticity of the brain and the fluidity of the mind in its effort to insure that survival will take place at whatever the cost. In so doing it narrows the range of perception so as to set up non-conflictual categories of self-experience as parts of the self (through the process of dissociation). Such is the language of trauma: a constricted narrative stitched together with great pain and effort, delineating what and how something must be remembered and told.

Notes

1 Current research has validated this and continues to study the neurobiology of attachment patterns, brain structure and intersubjectivity. For more on this please see Lainus (2025), Siegal (2024).

2 Since the analyst's regulating function is not independent of their co-participation, this echoes Winnicott's point that id relationships strengthen rather than disrupt a state of ego relatedness.

Part II

Chapter 5

Bromberg's Clinical Method and the Paradox of Technique

> It is only when an analyst holds his preferred stance as more than simply a personal sensibility—that is, as technique with a capital T, that he forecloses his ability to facilitate intersubjectivity and prevents his patient from using him optimally. The analyst must accept that his stance (no matter what it is) will eventually be met by a statement from some self-state of the patient that "This is not me" and you are not understanding who I am and what I need.
>
> (Bromberg, 2001)

Bromberg was deeply skeptical of the direct application of what we refer to as "technique" when it comes to the practice of interpersonal/relational analytic therapy, notwithstanding his enormous contribution to how it is practiced. While he made it clear that the application of "technique" in psychoanalysis or psychoanalytic therapy is better described as part of the problem, than part of any solution when it comes to therapy, we nevertheless believe that Bromberg contributed in highly significant ways to the development of what we think it would be fair to refer to as an interpersonal/intersubjective/relational "theory of technique."

While his skepticism regarding technique relates to an idea of applied technique as something brought into the therapy relationship from outside the borders of its process (as in the case of "manualized treatments), as a kind of Trojan Horse, his particular approach to clinical praxis is unmistakable. He developed a self-state-based approach to therapeutic work that was personal and particular enough that it could be described as "Brombergian," at the same

DOI: 10.4324/9781003381853-8

time that an integral part of his unique perspective stressed the dangers to therapeutic work of any direct "application of a technique" when participating in the "human relationship we call psychoanalysis" (Bromberg, 1996). This concern included a sense of the danger to the development of psychoanalysis itself as a function of working with "technique in mind," an orientation to clinical praxis that would threaten "losing the forest for the trees," or the patient for the theory.

His clinical perspective on praxis is a direct outgrowth of his theoretical and clinical emphasis on dissociation and the multiplicity of self-states, even as he minimized the role that theory plays in shaping the moment-to-moment experience of therapist and patient as they find their way toward a more fully alive, less dissociative, realer, more authentic experience that is one- of a kind. Spontaneity, the fostering of new experience and the possibility of safe enough surprises (2000, 2003), that can be tolerated and sponsor growth are the currency of Bromberg's approach to practice, and so the imposition on an unfolding, emergent practice of any kind of abstracted theoretical constructs in his view leads to more harm than good, and is likely to constitute an enactment of something taking place in the therapist and or patient that is beyond their joint awareness.

His approach to clinical practice was a phenomenological one, the experience of therapist and patient always at center stage, along with a recognition that much of human experience is dissociated, finding expression through enactment, and so not available to conscious awareness, including the experience of conflict or ambivalence. The effect of dissociative processes on human functioning, for better and worse, is a central element of what therapy addresses, in Bromberg's view, and what his method was designed to address.

His inquiries to his patients often took as their starting point his interest in what the patient's experience "is like," more so than about what something "meant," as any sense of felt meaning would have to await the greater self-awareness that would come with the diminishment of dissociation as a primary defense. His interest in what the patient could come to know about their experience included the experience of the therapist's participation: "What was it like for you when I did or said that," in an attempt to orient the patient's awareness to aspects of their felt experience that had been dissociated to that point, revealed by way of enactments that could destabilize the therapeutic relationship, before experience could be put into words. Such forms of destabilization constitute a point of departure for the patient and therapist to think about what had happened between them. The question of "what just happened here" or "between us" is often a starting point for fuller explorations of a patient's experience of self and other (therapist) that feels not so much a matter of "technique" as survival.

Bromberg's psychoanalytic sensibility, the personal and self-expressive use of the therapist's self (or selves) that he fostered through his work, as well as his clinical/theoretical emphasis on dissociation, multiple self-states, enactment, state sharing and self-revelation influenced several generations of analysts when it came to the way they worked, and so came to constitute a kind of clinical method in its own right. His therapeutic approach emphasized an ongoing negotiation between therapist and patients, as well as negotiation among the different self-states that each participant carries, in an intersubjective field of therapy. Such ongoing negotiations are emphasized in Bromberg's work in which the integrity of the authenticity of both participants, in their full multiplicity of self-states is privileged over any authority associated with the therapist's role or expertise.

Bromberg's emphasis on the therapy relationship as most essentially a subjective and intersubjective human experience of personal growth, self-expansion and healing, meant that the application of any given technique associated with any particular theoretical stance must come with a warning label: "It is only when an analyst holds his preferred stance as more than simply a personal sensibility—that is, as technique with a capital T, that he forecloses his ability to facilitate intersubjectivity and prevents his patient from using him optimally. The analyst must accept that his stance (no matter what it is) will eventually be met by a statement from some self-state of the patient that "This is not me, and you are not understanding who I am and what I need" (Bromberg, 2001).

For this reason, Bromberg believed that, continuing to think about what we do as technique, to the extent that technique suggests a way of working in which "expertise" is applied, slows the evolution of psychoanalysis, both clinically and as a body of theory, because the application of any general principle associated with a clinical theory of technique interferes with the fullest possible openness to the uniqueness of the patient and the therapist/patient dyad, threatening to interfere with the therapist's direct experience of his or her patient. The application of general principles threatens to create a kind of deafness to certain kinds of experience in which a therapist's theory can act as much a form of misdirection rather than offering the help to therapist and patient that its authors intended.

Bromberg described his view of the way a theory can distort a therapeutic process this way: "following a particular school of thought provides a valid frame for treatment, but the analyst's use of his subjective experience, above and beyond his theoretical loyalties, is the critical factor in promoting a patient's self-growth." The therapist's use and sharing of his or her own subjective experience fosters a reciprocal process that in turn, frees his or her patient's active involvement with the states of mind of the other. By engaging more fully with the mind of the therapist, made available to the patient through the therapist's "state sharing," a patient begins to experience his own dissociated self-states, at first through her encounter with the therapist's mind. Similarly, through her dedicated, self-reflective encounter with her patient in all the self-states that become manifest in their therapy conversations, the therapist too becomes familiar with parts of herself that have been inaccessible, or dissociated, to that point. The heart of the work, then, is the active and dedicated negotiation between subjectivities, not interpretation. This is to say that the therapist's attention to the intersubjective realms of experience that constitute the therapy relationship facilitates the patient's growth and the expansion of self-experience that expands self-awareness while minimizing the defensive use of dissociation that restricts it.

That is why Bromberg, in writing about "technique" in psychoanalytic work (2012), makes a strong case for "severing, or at the very least, further loosening our tie to that classical concept." The skill that the analyst brings to the situation "is not acquired through learned technique, nor is it applied." For Bromberg, growth in psychoanalysis is inherently relational—It embodies the relationship and takes place within it.

Given his central emphasis on the multiple subjectivities (expressive of different self-states) held by the two participants in any therapeutic encounter, any given application of a theory of technique that a therapist might draw on to a moment in therapy must be held loosely, with a humility born of the recognition of the ever-present blind spots and the multiplicity of self-state experiences always generating multiple views of the other and oneself, some true to one self-state in the foreground, others true to another self-state that for now occupies a position in the background. As one part of a patient feels recognized and understood by her therapist, another part stands by, perhaps feeling the sting of misrecognition, the shame of being dropped by her or his therapist, in favor of another part of her that for the moment occupies another state. The therapist is thus tasked with the role defining challenge of finding and maintaining contact with different parts of the patient, all at once. This involves finding points of identification and connection with more parts of the patient that may meet the eye at any one moment—the grown up successful, competent businessman who is telling me the story of a very good day at work, and the seven year old boy who feels like he can't compete with the "real" business man, or that he is about to be discovered for the fraud that he is and flooded with shame in the process. In seeing and hearing both the man in the boy and the boy in the man, I seek to find a way, as Bromberg showed, to show my hand over time (to show the patient what I see) in a way that allows both parts of the patient to find points of connection with me as well as with each other, in a way that clarifies their origin stories and eases the confusion and mystification that the patient feels in occupying multiple psychic positions at one time.

In the case of my patient Rob, as he described a victory at work in which he felt pride in the skills which allowed him to carry off a major negotiation, I could also feel the presence of the little boy who had seen his father "fall from grace," as he suddenly lost his position as a highly respected dean of a local college for reasons that were never clear, at least to the boy, and about which his parents were never explicit. He carried with him a vague feeling of scandal in the air, but he couldn't remember anyone inside or outside the home ever talking about it. His life changed dramatically after that. He recalled a moment in which he had come home to see his mother upset. When he asked what was wrong, she said "you are!" leaving him with a strong sense, an overwhelming feeling that his mother's upset had all been somehow his fault. As he spoke about feeling that he had been strong and successful at work, I could sense the little boy from that moment standing by, thinking that it was all about to go wrong, and it somehow would be his own fault. I said to him, "I think you are feeling worried that something will go terribly wrong, that this sense of finally coming into your own won't hold, and that you will feel that it is all your fault." At that point, feeling recognized by my comment, the little boy came to center stage, and was able to tell me more about how when he felt like he was being successful, it always felt (to him) like an act that he couldn't sustain for long. Someone would see through it, and he would be recognized for the scared little boy that he was. He told me about times in school in which he was bullied by the tougher boys, especially when they perceived him as being "too good or too smart." And how he would submit to their tortures because in some way he felt like "he had it coming." In taking note of another part of the patient standing by to provide more of the story, and inviting that younger boy to join in through my recognition of his presence, we were able to make room for more of that boy in the therapy, revealing more of his experience to me and to the other parts of himself as well.

Bromberg referred felicitously to such moments as reflecting the acquired "ability of the analyst to maintain dual citizenship in two domains of reality with passports to the multiple states of the patient." Of course, Bromberg recognized that as the therapist acquired the ability to maintain dual citizenship, the patient could begin to enjoy the benefits of greater freedom of citizenship in different parts of himself as well, allowing freer travel between states as well, and in so doing, begin to get to know more of himself and where he had been.

As we have emphasized, therapeutic choices boil down to what is useful to a particular analyst's work with a particular patient at a given point in time, as opposed to anything pre-determinable from the annals of clinical theory. In the case above, for example, I could have fashioned an Oedipal interpretation as a way of bringing the triangle of mother-father-son into focus emphasizing that an Oedipal victory in which he outdoes his dad and wins his mother's love, but I didn't think an interpretation would have captured the moment as well as staying closer to the phenomenology of this boy feeling that something was about to go all wrong. Still, considering what is useful to a particular patient at a particular time is never entirely knowable, because more than one perspective on the matter is always in the mix at the same time, and part of what is of therapeutic value is to help the patient to find ways of speaking up for the different perspectives held by different parts of himself, holding different truths in different domains of reality all at once. This is why decisions about what is useful to any given patient at any time cannot be made by one person alone (either patient or therapist), but rather constitute a kind of ongoing, work in process negotiation between not only the two participants in therapy, but also different parts of each person that might find one or another form of participation most useful.

Bromberg emphasized that in an analytic relationship, it is impossible to unravel, or even clearly distinguish what is personal from what is professional. The psychoanalytic relationship is first and foremost a personal, deeply intimate relationship, notwithstanding its status as a professional relationship agreed upon by both its participants as a way to help the patient to heal, to change and to grow. In Bromberg's emphasis on the personal dimension of psychoanalytic work the concept of technique feels not just unnecessary, but a hindrance to the work of psychotherapy by which it is defined. Since the work as Bromberg sees it invites a self-reflective recognition of another's subjectivity, at the same time that the therapist remains as attuned as possible to his or her own (and the intersubjective field that these two subjectivities create in their encounter with one another), any preconceived "technical" orientation to the work would seem to be at cross purposes with the intention to reside in and follow the experience that emerges as the therapeutic relationship unfolds.

Bromberg's placement of subjectivity and intersubjectivity at the heart of the project, analytic anything resembling "technique," or a theory of praxis, regardless of the school of thought from which it is derived, is useful only if it is not held as objectively "correct," but rather expressive of something about the therapist that the patient is free to have her own feelings about (2006a, p. 71).

From a classical perspective, such a moment might be viewed as a form of resistance—the patient is not able to or refused to take in or to recognize what the therapist is rightly trying to bring to her attention. From a Kleinian perspective, the patient's refusal to recognize what the therapist is telling her about the contents of her mind might be seen as an "attack on linking," or an attack on the analyst's mind and thinking process. From Bromberg's perspective, a part of the patient is identifying herself in her statement that "this is not *me*." You may be speaking to another part of me, and I have been listening to *that* conversation, but now I would like to tell you how *I* am responding to what you are saying, and how *I* am seeing *you* in light of that.

Bromberg believed that while each psychoanalytic school of thought provides a frame for treatment that has been useful for therapists of *that* persuasion, the analyst's use of his subjective experience, above and beyond his theoretical loyalties, is the critical factor in promoting a patient's self-growth.

In his view "the analyst's use of his own subjective experience fosters a reciprocal process that in turn, frees the patient's active involvement with the states of mind of the other, and in so doing, the patient is able, sometimes for the first time, '*speak her own mind*'." This reciprocity allows a patient to begin to experience the self-states that are dissociated but are being held in the mind of the other. The heart of the work at that point is the negotiation between subjectivities, not interpretation.

Bromberg's complex and paradoxical relationship to the art of technique is captured in the following statement. As Bromberg put it:

> When I am with a patient, myself experience is so highly organized through the relationship that being an analyst feels like being myself. Since I do not experience myself as doing analysis any more than I experience myself as doing any relationship, the concept of technique does not enhance my understanding of what shapes the self I bring to an analytic relationship

(2012)

However, Bromberg goes on to clarify, that "as an analyst, the manner in which I am being myself is shaped by guiding principles even though they represent how I am, rather than strategic acts that I do. These ways of being are part of the relationship rather than techniques implemented within it, but they do indeed represent my analyst-self in ways that do not shape the self I bring to other relationships. Things are said and done by my analyst-self that would not be said or done by me in other relationships."

For Bromberg, an essential ingredient of a therapy relationship is spontaneity, along with a dedicated attention to the sense of psychic safety of as many parts of the patient, in as many different self-states as possible. At the same time, Bromberg recognized that complete safety in the presence of another person is not possible for most people/most patients—constituting in most cases an illusion that would leave some parts of the patient unrecognized, curtailing opportunity for those parts of the patient to find personal expression.

Bromberg turned his attention, then, to the act of living in and with the self-reflective tension that inevitably arises when "standing in the spaces" between states that enable spontaneity with those that attend to the risk involved when parts of the patients feel unsafe, when the spontaneity of the analyst is experienced by the patient, or some part of the patient, as inattentive to or unrecognizing of some of her needs.

Bromberg (2001) described his work with "Helen," a patient in her mid-30s:

> who had a history of severe trauma that had led to a reliance on dissociation so long-standing that she was unable to experience herself with a past that felt like hers, a present that she breathed life into, or a future that she could imagine. To ensure that the protective function of her dissociative solution remained reliable, she had defined the scope of her existence in a manner so limiting that she allowed herself almost no interchange with the outside world other than her work.

We will quote his description of his work with Helen at some length, as it provides a window into Bromberg's attention to the therapeutic possibilities that unfold between therapist and patient in the spontaneity of relations to the benefit of both participants:

> When I first met her, she could barely contain her unprocessed rage at knowing that she was somehow shortchanged as a human being but not knowing who to blame or whether she even had the right to do so. "Was I just born this way—different from everyone else—or could I have been a whole person if only …?" Ironically, she was herself a therapist—a therapist endowed with an extraordinary gift for healing others despite her own pain, which never went away. Being a therapist, she was aware that I wrote, and she made a point to read my work as it appeared in print. I was never quite sure of what she did with what she read, because the impact of experiencing me as part of "the world out there" was held in different domains of reality by different parts of her self, and I was privy only to those parts that were least likely to threaten the fragility of the attachment that she felt was always in danger of being irreparably broken … After about five years of work, we had reached a point at which she was able to hold in conscious awareness the existence of her own dissociative processes and was able to reflect on what function they served. Not surprisingly, she also began to share with me aspects of herself that were now safer to allow into our relationship, including her growing ability to make self-reflective use of some of my writings in a way that was dramatically different from her storing them away as a protection against discovering their existence unexpectedly and being helpless to prevent their assault on her mind.
>
> On this particular day, she arrived for her session filled with undisguised enthusiasm—a state that caught me completely unprepared, as I had not been part of it before. I blurted out both my surprise and delight, but withheld my confusion, hoping she wouldn't see it. She responded, however, with a mischievous smile, and said that for a change it was me who had to deal with being shocked, and that it made her feel strong to have read my writing without feeling she was doing something bad either to me or to herself.

"In fact," she went on, "I'm enjoying the disturbed look on your face; there's something about it that makes me feel closer to you." She then reported having just read my latest paper, thinking about it, and experiencing an exciting insight about herself—as she put it, "without help from *anyone.*"

As I began to reply, I found myself aware of speaking from a strange state of mind in which I felt more like her patient than her therapist—a state that, uncannily, was as physical as it was mental. I was clearly not "myself"—at least not any of the selves I was accustomed to being when I was with her. Oddly, I wasn't anxious about the shift in our roles, and was even aware of feeling "held" by her self-confident recognition of what was taking place. In retrospect, I'm pretty sure that this was a part of why I hadn't been anxious—it *felt good.*

Is this, I wondered, what she is like in her own office? If so, small wonder her patients get better. As I allowed myself to more and more "go with" my "unboundaried" feeling of intimacy, I could sense that my own spontaneity was being matched by a new level of spontaneity in her and that we were in fact experiencing aspects of each other's selves with an immediacy that had not before been possible.

Later, when reflecting on how much I had enjoyed the moment, I recalled a remark by Haley (1993, cited in Bromberg, 2001b) about Carl Whitaker: "He most enjoyed a treatment session when he could say afterward, 'I never did that before'" (p. 15).

As it typical of Bromberg's descriptions of therapeutic process, no word is ever the last word.

One state gives way to another, as the patient slowly begins to occupy a place in between. The experience of something new gives way to the experience and clarification of something old.

Helen's experience of her own spontaneity in the moment with her therapist led to the following insight into a different state in which her experience had been restricted:

"I now understand," Helen said, "why I am always making pronouncements to you about how I'm going to be different, but never act on them. It's a way that when I'm with you In can get past the corner but still be me—the me that's safe. While I'm with you in a session, what's around the corner is safe because you're there, so I make a pronouncement about how I'm going to be different tomorrow because today isn't tomorrow. But then when tomorrow comes I'm all by myself and I can't remember ever feeling safe."

Of course, analytic therapists of various persuasions would agree that the relationship between therapist and patient is a crucial starting point for therapy, that establishing a good and solid "therapeutic alliance" is one of the first orders of business in beginning therapeutic work, The therapist makes use of the solid base for therapeutic relating so formed in sustaining the arduous and winding road of therapy to a conclusion in which the patient is better off for his or her efforts.

For Bromberg, though, the development of the relationship between therapist and patient, the way that it comes to be and what and how each partner contributes to its troubles, their a ways of being stuck and their finding their way back to some sense of movement and growth—this is the therapy itself. It embodies the therapy rather than being the first order of business in initiating a therapy relationship that has another agenda.

Chapter 6

Bromberg and the Art of Listening

> Bromberg (personal communication) described a moment in which he felt moved, seemingly out of the blue, to ask his patient about her experience of having her mother read to her. He couldn't say what moved him to ask—just a feeling he had—he didn't know what he had heard or seen. It could have been a subtle shift in the tone of her voice, or the tilt of her head, that brought the intimate image of a mother and child to his mind, an uncanny moment of deep attunement in which he could feel the patient's mother in the room in a way that brought moments of their early relationship back to her mind that had been lost to history in the trauma of her loss.

The art of listening was a central focus in Bromberg's work. Whether in his therapeutic work, his teaching, supervising, or consulting, his attention to the listening process itself was of paramount importance. First and foremost, the analyst listens. Everything we do and say as analysts follows from how we listen, and what our listening in the way that we do brings us to hear, and to see. Bromberg's 1994 paper, "Speak, that I may see you," explored the act of listening at the heart of the therapeutic project. Our patients speak so that they may be found, even as parts of them remain silent in their hiding places, hoping to elude us. Sometimes speech is itself elusive, challenging the therapist to look beyond spoken words to other sources of the patient's truth—between the lines or in action.

"Listening" is of course fundamental to the work of all psychoanalysts. But not all analysts listen alike, just as no two

DOI: 10.4324/9781003381853-9

painters paint alike. Artists use different color pallets, different brush strokes, and are recognized by the style of their "school" even as each artist associated with that school is *sui generis*. Similarly, psychoanalytic ways of listening are not all alike, even as they share qualities that are different from other ways of listening. Analysts listen to their friends, spouses, and children differently from the way they listen to their patients. Yet even when it comes to listening to their patients, no two analysts listen in just the same way. And even a single analyst listens differently with each patient, since even our ways of listening are themselves co-created by therapist and patient together.

The way we listen, patient and therapist alike, bears the unique stamp of the mind of the listener, conscious and unconscious, associated and dissociated, at that moment in time, together with the patient (or therapist) that shares the listening space. As therapy develops over time, it is shaped by the psychic choreography of two listening and speaking subjects, whose growing capacity to listen to self and other is a crucial marker of therapeutic progress. "Speak, that I may see you," the title of Bromberg's 1994 paper on dissociation, reality, and psychoanalytic listening, reflects the truth that we see each other through the lens of what we can hear as we listen. I see you as I listen to you, and as I speak you see me too. And what I hear informs what I see (Bromberg, 1991; Khan, 1971), just as what I see informs what I hear. Listening takes place through all the known senses and beyond. For Bromberg, therapy takes place in a perceptual field in which the therapist seeks to expand the field of seeing and hearing for therapist and patient over time, as dissociative processes make way for the actualization of associative potentials.

Nothing defines a therapist's personal, unique way of working, his therapeutic sensibility, and way of participating in the process more than how they listen. The question of how an analyst listens, what they hear, and how they make use of it is fundamental to Bromberg's way of working. Listening, after all, is the starting point for all psychoanalytic work, and how we listen is the first quality of our participation that our patients experience and relate to. Our patients hear, see, and experience us through the ways that we listen. When a patient feels that we "listen well," their therapy has a chance to be helpful over time, as little by little more parts of the patient will feel safe enough to make their appearance in the therapy. When we fail to hear our patients, or parts of them, as we inevitably will do, we try to open our minds to their correction in the ways in which we listen, and when we succeed, we hear and see more.

Bromberg's placement of "listening" squarely at his center of attention regarding the analyst's ways of participating in the therapeutic process was reflected in his naming of the courses and seminars he taught on the psychoanalytic process of simply "Listening." These seminars placed listening itself as the object of study, as the first and most essential function that the therapist brings to the work. Bromberg's listening seminars were a fundamental part of the training of candidates at the NYU Postdoctoral Program, the William Alanson White Institute, the Institute for Contemporary Psychoanalysis in New York, and elsewhere for a half century, reflecting his emphasis on listening with his unique (at the time, in psychoanalytic training programs) use of audio tapes of therapy sessions as the centerpiece of the seminar process. Generations of therapists had the experience of listening along with Bromberg and their seminar mates to the music of therapy sessions, a form of ear training that informs my way of listening to this day. I have adopted this model of using taped sessions to study listening (to our patients and to ourselves simultaneously), in order to expand the realm of what it is possible for us to hear, from the inside and out.

Bromberg's (and later my) seminars were organized such that the presenter would share a tape of a recent session, and they and the other seminar participants would "just listen." After listening for a while, everyone would reflect on their experience of listening, and share what they heard (between the lines) as they listened to both therapist and patient, and of course, the inner music produced. No two seminar participants heard the session the same way. Each therapist had their own way of listening, their unique listening attitude revealing different aspects of the patient, and of course, themselves. Each participant would hear something different, would tune into a different quality of the experience, a different tone, a different current of feeling or thought that would bring each of us to imagine a different patient, a different session. Each participant would bring a different quality of listening to the experience, and the different ways of listening brought different qualities of the patient, the therapist, and the therapy to light.

Theodor Reik was a favorite author of Bromberg's; his 1949 book *Listening with the Third Ear* a common point of reference in his teaching and thinking. Following Reik's metaphor, Bromberg emphasized listening with one's whole being, as fully present as it was possible to be, with the "third ear" metaphor capturing the essence of the listening process standing for the way in which the therapist's unconscious oriented to the sounds of the patient's. No two therapists hear the patient in exactly the same way, because each of them plays a different "instrument," an instrument tuned to the sounds of one's own unconscious as well as that of the patient. The patient comes to know the therapist in their ways of hearing and knowing.

With the full range of intersubjective dimensions of therapeutic work highlighting the uniqueness of each dyad that was central to Bromberg's approach and sensibility, he brought a highly focused kind of attention in his way of listening to the full palette of his patient's experience, including his patient's experience of how the analyst participated in the work. "What does it feel like to be with me (the therapist) in any given moment?" Such attention brought to the forefront different parts of the patient, as each moment could catch the drift of the experience of a different part of the patient, and in so doing inevitably gave new voice to the patient's experience of different parts of the therapist.

Bromberg's emphasis on listening with an ear to the ground concerning how different parts of the patient respond to different parts of the therapist was sure to bring surprises to therapist and patient alike when the conditions in the therapeutic relationship were safe enough to bear it. It is the therapist's capacity that develops over time with each patient, to listen to their patient's experience of the therapist even when what they hear is unexpected and unwelcome (when the patient hears and experiences parts of the therapist that the therapist would rather not see) that moves the therapy forward.

Bromberg's seminars were not meant to foster the development of any particular "technical" stance or orientation per se, but rather to study in as much detail as possible the process of listening itself, since everything a therapist does and says follows from their way of listening, and what it allows them to hear. His emphasis on the "third ear" highlighted the fact that listening is not a function of the ears alone. We listen through all our known senses and those not yet mapped, as we attend to what is arising in ourselves and strive to find parts of our patient as yet unknown.

His listening seminars put a fine point on listening itself as the essential skill that a therapist brings to the work, as members would practice listening not just to the words but to the music of the sessions, including the sounds of silence in the spaces between the words, the quality of the spaces between the words, and the sounds and tones of the words themselves. We "heard" that no two silences sound or feel the same. Some feel quiet and relaxing, a comfortable and comforting space in which to be together without intrusion, when words aren't necessary. Other silences were noisy, even strident, and abandoning. We could "hear" the difference by listening to ourselves in the silence; did we feel quiet in the silence, or did we feel a roar of the blood rushing through our ears? In the case of the latter, we may find our way into aspects of the exchange that have been laying low in an enacted dimension that has not yet seen the light of day in the therapeutic conversation.

Bromberg's seminars might have been called "essential listening exercises in therapy," a music appreciation seminar of a kind where the music is that of the therapy itself. The seminar members practiced listening to the patient being presented, the therapist presenting, and all the members of the seminar who were hearing the music their own way. We all heard something different, and what we would imagine saying and doing flowed directly from the music. This is an approach that I have adapted in my own seminars and workshops, starting with the one I (AB) began to teach at the Institute of Contemporary Psychoanalysis in New York after Philip Bromberg stepped down from teaching the class in 1990. We could all see how being in "the grip of the field" made hearing some sounds impossible, because hearing them would have required a recognition of parts of the patient or parts of the therapist that were not yet ready to be known ("not-me" parts) as Bromberg would say, drawing on Sullivan's designation that became integral to the Interpersonal Tradition and its early emphasis on dissociation—of parts of the self that could not be recognized as part of "me." The power of shame, an essential part of what dissociation serves to modulate in order to manage the disorganizing dysregulation that it brings, is ever present in the therapy dyad, strongly affecting how both the patient and therapist are able to listen to each other and what they can hear. Listening is compromised by dissociation, for patient and therapist alike. The therapist's dawning awareness of the ways that his or her listening is compromised, as when an enactment is underway, redirects her attention to the source of the restriction, giving the therapist access to self that had been closed off or entangled with complementary parts of the patient.

The therapist's interventions are always an expression of how they listen, and what they hear; what they hear is an expression of what the therapist has access to and what they do not, because "not-me" parts of the therapist will make hearing harder in at least one ear. What they bring to the session by way of prior learning and preferred theoretical perspectives will contribute to the therapist's way of listening, for better or worse; worse because expectations borne of theoretical preconceptions can minimize the surprise that can come of regarding another person with fresh eyes and ears. Each therapist brings their own sensitivities to the work, as well as their own limits and blind spots. What we think we already know about the patient, and how to best respond to what they bring from our sojourns in psychoanalytic theory, will inevitably orient the listener to some degree, but what we hear based on our expectations (including our theoretical perspectives) must be taken with a grain of salt since any expectations based on a preferred stance or theory is as likely to serve as static, an interference to listening in a fully present way—something that may stand between the patient and the therapist's ability to hear something new, to be surprised, which is essential to psychoanalytic change, as Bromberg emphasized.

Listening with a radical openness to being surprised (a version of Bion's dictum to listen without memory or desire) sensitizes the therapist to changes in voice and idiom that orient them to parts of the patient, other voices, that they might otherwise not identify, as they fade into the background, with the potential to bring confusion and mystification to both participants. My patient tells me a story that I have heard before, but the voice tone, or the breath, or the tilt of the head is a bit different. I notice that the story that I had before begins to feel like a different story, one told from a different point of view. Something in the story about which the patient and I had shared a laugh before, now seems terribly sad, and I notice that tears begin to stream down my patient's face as his mother, who had seemed silly, laughable, in a previous version of the story, now seemed pathetic. Now the patient experienced some shame about the "heartlessness" with which he had told it before. I noticed a tear in my own eye as well, as I too felt something different, much more poignant than my feeling had been in previous tellings of the "same" story. "Why had I joined in with the laughter before," I wondered. But then it occurred to me that it was actually a different story, as it was told from a different part of the patient and received by a different part of me. The story was now not so much about his mother but one expressing his sense that he should have been kinder to her, more attuned to her own trauma, rather than laughing along with his brothers and father at her expense.

Bromberg's orientation to a way of listening with disciplined sensitivity to self-state changes that occur in both patient and therapist were central to his method. In his attunement to the presence of different parts of the patient making their presence felt in the relationship with his patient, Bromberg would take pains to acknowledge their presence, to welcome each part of the patient that would appear over time and in turn. If not explicitly stated, though often it was, it amounted to an acknowledgment of a new presence in the therapy, implicitly in tone of voice or in a warm look, if not explicitly stated—"Welcome, come on in, it is good to meet you. I have the sense that you have a different feeling about this than I have known about before."

The essence of Bromberg's (interpersonal relational) listening stance turns the classical way of listening on its head. The defining quality that distinguished it from evenly hovering attention is that the analyst's overarching attunement is to his contextualized perceptual experience; verbal content is one ingredient of the here and now perceptual field—an ever-changing field that is shaped by a felt disjunction between what is being enacted and what is being said.

> In an interpersonal/relational listening stance (Bromberg, 1998a, 1998b, 1998c, 2006a, 2006b, 2009), the analyst's overarching state of mind is attuned to his fluctuating, moment to moment experience of what it is like for him to be with his patient and for his patient to be with him during the course of the session, particularly along the dimension of affect regulation and dysregulation. It is a stance in which his perception of constantly shifting, multiple perspectives—his own and his patient's, are the source of the raw data, the material.
>
> (Bromberg, 2012)

His emphasis on listening with self-states in mind, rather than from a singular center of self, requires an overarching attunement to whoever is speaking, with a recognition that every patient is comprised of multiple speakers. A therapist listens in a way that allows recognition of the appearance and disappearance of these different voices, the different parts of a patient that comprise their full self. For any human being, feeling differently at different moments about the same thing, or getting into a mood, represents a shift to a state of consciousness with its own internal integrity, its own reality, and its own truth (1996, p. 255).

The challenge for an analyst that Bromberg's work highlights and addresses is to sustain an awareness that with every patient some state shifts have a minimal link or no link to other states of consciousness, even to those that may have just preceded the change. How does an analyst listen to these moments in which the absence of a link between states of consciousness is revealed? Illustrating this point, he describes a patient who, having been reading a book in bed, looks down at the book, noticing that it was wet. Only then did the patient realize that she had been crying. Bromberg asks, "what allows the analyst to comfortably conceptualize the fact that she didn't know she had been crying *when* it was happening? Does he think of such a mundane event as even interesting, analytically?" (1996, p. 509). How does an analyst listen to what the patient is telling him in recounting the story?

Another example, from Bromberg's 1996 paper, "Standing in the Spaces": "A patient, a woman with an eating disorder, is asked by her analyst to describe the details of last night's binge. She cannot do it. She insists, in a voice without affect, that she has no memory of the step-by-step experience of what she ate, how she ate it, and what she thought or felt as she was eating." Does the analyst hear this as "resistance?" he asks.

> A new referral, perhaps an unanticipated dissociative identity disorder (formerly known as multiple personality), enters a trance state during an analytic session and, seemingly spontaneously, enacts a vivid portrayal of a child in the midst of a horrifying event, and then has no memory of that part of the session. How does the analyst perceive the "trance" phenomenon and his patient's subsequent report of amnesia for the event that had taken place before the analyst's eyes just a few moments before? From what stance shall the analyst attempt to engage the patient about any or all of this?
>
> A patient is engaged in a passionate sexual moment that she refers to, in session, as "coming in diamonds." She and her lover are "lost" in each other, and she, a woman who had entered analysis with "gender confusion," has a visual experience that her lover's penis, moving in and out, might be his or might be hers. She can't tell "whose penis it is, who is fucking whom," and "it doesn't matter." How does the analyst hear and process this "loss of reality testing" at that moment?

How does an analyst listen to his patients at such moments?

Bromberg (personal communication) described a moment in which he felt moved, seemingly out of the blue, to ask his patient about her experience of having her mother read to her. He couldn't say what moved him to ask—just a feeling he had—he didn't know what he had heard or seen. It could have been a subtle shift in the tone of her voice, or the tilt of her head, that brought the intimate image of a mother and child to his mind, an uncanny moment of deep attunement in which he could feel the patient's mother in the room in a way that brought moments of their early relationship back to her mind that had been lost to history in the trauma of her loss. How had Bromberg detected the presence of the patient's mother in the room at that moment, leading him, for reasons he himself did not know, to ask about the intimate moment? The image came, as he was able to reconstruct it later, by way of a reverie of tender, precious moments with his own mother, an image that came to mind as he listened to his patient. Had the patient evoked Bromberg's childhood memory by way of her own "state," which contained a reference to her childhood experience, out of awareness until Bromberg, who had gotten the message by way of his own self-state shift, called the question? Was the tilt of her head, and a look of rapt attention on her face that evoked a sense memory of his own that transported him to the warm, exquisite feeling that he had while listening to his mother as she read to him. As he found the memory of his mother reading to the three-year-old boy that he was, the happiest time of his childhood while in the presence of his patient, he found that he was drawn to imagine his patient—with an image of her three-year-old child self that mirrored his own, making possible the uncanny query that brought her mother (and his) back to life all these years later.

In finding his patient's mother sitting by quietly in the session, he was able to find the little girl basking in the love of the story hour, and eventually to be able to reclaim the lost mother and feelings associated with her loss, bringing much more of his patient to life, along with the parts of him that had received the message calling them forth.

Subtle shifts in a patient's tone of voice, the cadence of their speech, the cadence of breath, alert the therapist to changes in the patient's states of consciousness, or the dysregulation of affect states that are not yet subject to formulation by either member of the therapeutic couple.

If an analyst thinks of a person as speaking from different self-states rather than from a single center of self, then the analyst will inevitably listen that way. That is at the heart of Bromberg's way of listening, involving a special attunement to both the impact the speaker (patient) is having on you at any given moment and the *shifts* in that impact as close to the time they occur as possible.

Bromberg's description of his work with Ernest (2006a, p. 35) captures an aspect of his way of listening, to the patient and to himself at the same time, and speaking from the place that such listening makes possible. This generates a special form of authentic and generative contact that brings parts of the patient and parts of the therapist into awareness in new ways, constituting a crucial aspect of the therapeutic actions itself. As Bromberg described (2006a, pp. 35–36):

> Ernest entered treatment with a history of "failed" sexual conquests. Women who initially seemed interested in him romantically very shortly (usually on the first date) found an excuse to not see him again. Ernest was a man whose capacity for dissociation was so extreme that his inertia was sometimes almost unbearable. He could literally not allow a here-and-now experience of aliveness with another human being to exist for more than a few moments. Intersubjective give-and-take was seemingly unknowable to him.
>
> I can recall the first time I felt a moment of authentic contact between the two of us as real people. He was recounting another of his dissociated ventures into dating and said, in his usual robotlike delivery, "Every time I ask a woman to go to sleep with me, she turns me down." Something in that moment, perhaps my need to avoid recognizing my own hypnoid trance (sometimes called boredom) made me attend to Ernest's use of language more carefully than I might have otherwise.
>
> Your choice of words just struck me … You described how you asked a woman to "go to sleep with you." I think, though I'm not completely certain, that the typical way of putting it is "asking a woman to sleep with you." I wonder if that difference might be important. When you ask someone to "go to sleep with you" it usually means what it literally sounds like it means—going to sleep. When you ask someone to "sleep with

you," it is usually understood to mean an invitation to engage in sex. I have a feeling that your use of language may involve more than just a lack of familiarity with the right words.

"What do you mean?" asked Ernest, speaking as from a cave below the ground. As I was about to "explain" what I meant with another torrent of words, the boring quality of my own words made me "wake up." I chose instead to respond with what I was experiencing at that moment. I was flooding him with words and could well understand if he could not get what I was talking about. I then wondered aloud whether my nonstop wordiness might be my way, unconsciously, of trying to deal with something I was not letting myself recognize was happening between us: we were talking to each other as if we were on separate islands, each alone in his own space with no way to connect personally to each other.

He asked again what I meant. This time I felt more connected. I replied that I might have been trying to overcome my feeling of being all by myself by substituting words—a lot of words for the personal contact I really wanted and could feel some of right now, but had kind of given up hope of having without realizing it. I wondered if this made any sense to him in terms of his own experience of what had just happened between us.

He allowed that my explanation actually was very close to what he felt but he was not really aware that he felt it until I said it. He continued, hesitantly, saying that my using the word personal scared him and made him feel that he was not understanding me again. But he knew that what I was saying was true, and he, too, felt hopeless about it ever being different because that was just who he is. I asked if what I had said to him wanting to get closer to him may have felt like more than he could handle at that moment. I wondered aloud if perhaps his wish not to "understand" me was a wish to lower the volume of his feelings by moving himself to a safer place—a safe island inside his own head where he could talk without having to risk being flooded by more than his mind could deal with. I said I knew I might be scaring him by just asking this, but that I wanted to try anyway. Ernest then revealed, for the first time, that he lived in a state of terror and that everything he did in his life was a way of appearing as if he were like everyone else while knowing that he was just pretending. He always hoped that I would show him how to do the right way what others seemed to do so easily. He said that he was scared at that moment but that he was glad that he could at least say this much.

Was this enactment a turning point? I don't know. Perhaps the "real" turning point had already happened and this was just the fallout.

I guess I really do believe that change precedes insight. Yes, he did then start to think about the fact that in the act of trying to relate to another human being, whether a date or an analyst, he usually shifts to a self-state that is as deadened to the immediacy of here and now aliveness that he literally forces the other person either to "go to sleep with him," or to retreat into an equally boring and impersonal exchange of words.

In hearing his patient's expression "every time I ask a woman to go to sleep with me," Bromberg was awakened from his own sleepy trance with the recognition that his patient's way of being actually had the capacity to put a date, as well as an analyst, to sleep. This was far from the kind of intimate contact that the patient believed he sought despite the fact that it continuously eluded him. Bromberg's listening to Ernest in such a way that made possible a point of entry to an aspect of the patient's experience that had been hidden in the fog that the patient had cast upon the therapy made possible an exchange in which his patient's vulnerability could be found as the fog cleared enough to see it, as the patient could begin to see what he had contributed all along to the elusiveness of real contact with another person.

Bromberg may not have been providing Ernest exactly what he thought he needed (for Bromberg to show him how do be able to do what he believed others could do so easily), but in the work that they were doing together, in Bromberg's listening between the lines and speaking from there, Ernest was able to find his way to locate himself between the lines, keeping parts of himself cordoned off from others, as he could begin to put words to his longing and vulnerability for the first time. As he began to do that, he could begin to speak without putting himself and others to sleep.

In the next chapter we will further consider the clinical implications of this way of listening, which directs the therapist's attention to working with dissociation and the multiplicity of self-state experience in mind.

Chapter 7

Dissociation, Multiplicity, Enactment, and Self-State Work

The Heart of Bromberg's Clinical Method

> Once the concept of dissociation becomes entrenched within a therapist's clinical imagery, the hermeneutic process of analysis is shaped neither by interpretation nor by interaction per se, but by the analyst's effort "to maintain dual citizenship in two domains of reality, with passports to multiple self-states of the patient."
>
> (Bromberg, 1991, p. 410)

As we have seen, a model of the mind that recognizes the centrality of dissociative processes in all human beings, on a spectrum from normality to severe illness, is a key to Bromberg's approach to psychotherapeutic work, and the development of his clinical theory. With ordinary as well as more extreme (usually early) forms of trauma-based dissociative phenomena in mind, including most notably the multiplicity of self-state experience that trauma-based dissociation engenders, the therapist tries to stay attuned, as much as possible, to the ways in which the patient (and therapist) occupy different and ever-shifting self-states over time in the therapeutic relationship. When this occurs in the course of a single session in which different self-states make their appearance and occupy center stage in kaleidoscopic fashion, while others remain in the background awaiting their turn to claim self-expression and recognition, this poses special challenges as well as opportunities for therapist and patient alike. It frequently leads to confusion and enactments as the therapist is challenged to follow and respond with as much of a sense of recognition as it is possible to find in a given moment to multiple voices in the patient, responding to each

DOI: 10.4324/9781003381853-10

part of the patient in its own terms. As one part of the patient comes to feel recognized, another is likely to feel invisible and aggrieved, as different parts of the patient have different stories to tell, different memories carrying different affective states, understandings, and perspectives linked to different developmental stages and a cacophony of experiences that have remained sequestered from one another until the therapy work enables some linking of the states, or at least some beginning recognition of one another's presence, made possible through their recognition by the therapist.

The therapist, in responding to self-state shifts that occur in a session with as finely attuned recognition of each voice in its own right as is possible, allows further elaboration together with the patient of the experience held in each state in turn, enabling the patient over time to feel increasingly recognized in and by all of their different parts, and ways of being. Over time, this minimizes the need for the activation of extreme dissociative defenses, as the consequences of a potentially traumatic encounter between oneself state, or part of the self, and another become increasingly less threatening, dire, and disorganizing.

Bromberg showed how the identification of the danger, the repetition of its traumatic affect, as re-enactments of the trauma scenes occur within the therapy relationship; the eventual softening of the traumatic effect can occur in a therapeutic relationship as a result of the therapist's capacity to respond to the different parts of the patient in turn and in ways that reflect their good enough recognition, a feat made possible in part by the therapist's careful attention to their own shifts in self-state while in the presence of the patient. Such recurring and often linked (between therapist and patient) shifts in state constitute in part a form of unconscious communication between patient and therapist that enables the therapist to come to know the patient "from the inside out" (1991), an aspect of what Bromberg refers to as "the aesthetics of unconscious communication."

This process of identifying and responding with the fullest possible recognition and empathy to the changing array of characters within a person poses no small challenge to a therapist, especially when the different parts of the patient that come into play in the field of therapy have been unfamiliar to or unrecognized by the therapist, sometimes for long periods of time before they make their appearance; or when the therapist is finally able to take note of their presence as they become manifest in a disruptive and disturbing enactment or when the therapist's own dissociation of such states has fended off disturbing responses to them that would come back with a vengeance with their recognition.

It is often the case, especially early in an analysis, that different self-states in the patient have been out of touch with each other, unaware of one another's presence, as a result of the fragmentation of the self that is a response to trauma. The matter of how a therapist attends to different parts of a patient and the states that they occupy, and responds to each in its own terms, is complicated in the therapeutic situation by the fact that the therapist has their own shifting self-states to contend with; some of these are more familiar to the therapist than others, and often triggered by those of the patient, which contributes to the difficulty that any given therapist might have staying in touch with parts of the patient, for reasons of their own.

Since the therapist, like the patient, occupies states that are to varying degrees dissociated (out of awareness, or disconnected from the primary state that he or she is aware of occupying at the time), their responses, and/or their source in the psyche of the therapist, may also be subject to dissociative processes. When this is the case, they are prone to manifest themselves in the therapy situation in the form of enactments, which may lead the therapist and patient to eventually realize that there has been more going on between them, and within them, than has met the eyes of either of the participants in the process, making possible its verbal expression and symbolization (the recognition of meaning beyond what is manifest in the most concrete terms) for the first time.

In this way, enactments in therapy, traditionally understood to be problematic in therapy and to be avoided whenever possible (with the help of further analysis and supervision), are now understood, as by Bromberg, to be a crucial part of the therapeutic action; a most important part of a process by which dissociated parts of the patient become available to joint awareness, and for joint reflection by both therapist and patient that can lead to a better understanding of how some parts of the patient have become unmoored from other parts.

This fundamental aspect of Bromberg's method, emphasizing the crucial contribution of the therapist's finely tuned attention to his own self-states, states of consciousness, affective states, body states, and moods in the presence of the patient as a primary source of information informing the therapist about aspects of the patient's experience that have eluded their or the patient's awareness to that point is similar to Bollas's (1983) description of the way the therapist must look to find the patient in themselves:

> by cultivating a freely roused emotional sensibility the analyst welcomes news from within himself that is reported through his own hunches, feeling states, passing images, fantasies and imagined interpretive interventions .... It is a feature of our present day understanding of the transference, that the Other source of the analysand's free associations is the psycho-analyst's contertransference, so much so that to find the patient we must look for him in ourself.
>
> (p. 2)

Bromberg's recognition of the underground springs of connection between the psychic experience of patient and therapist and the use of such linkages to find parts of the patient split off from their awareness at that time mirrored, too, the findings that Ferenczi reported on in his 1932 Clinical Diary (Dupont, 1988; Bromberg, 1991; Bass, 2015) in his discovery of a "dialogue of unconsciouses" that constituted a constant presence "alongside" or "underneath" the conscious conversation taking place between therapist and patient.

For Bromberg, his recognition that there were always at least two patients in the room (and more, because each therapist and each patient is comprised of many therapists and patients, each of which takes their turn in center stage over time) meant that "state sharing," the intentional reflective "self-revelation" or "self-disclosure" of aspects of the therapist's self-experience while in the presence of the patient constituted an essential part of his method.

Through the personal sharing of the therapist's states of mind, the patient often finds their way to the recognition of their own (Bromberg, 1993, 2006a, 2006b, 2008), because their states of mind are often interconnected in a kind of matrix of linked states such that the elaboration and clarification of one person's states of mind can lead to a complementary elaboration and clarification of the others'. Dissociated states of mind of the patient arouse like or complementary states of mind in the therapist, sometimes becoming entangled in what amounts to a kind of knot that is experienced as an impasse, what Wolstein (1992) referred to as an interlock of transference and countertransference. Bromberg (2006a, 2006b) emphasized that attending to one forges a path toward the awareness of the other, and so saw the analyst's self-revelation as a crucial part of the process of turning impasse and enactment into a more free flowing associative encounter.

The process of following the trails that become evident as therapy unfolds and locating the multiple self-states of each participant (therapist and patient alike) in every psychoanalytic project means that lines may be blurred between therapist and patient, supervisor and supervisee, each of whom is a decentered subject with multiple-state based points of view in the service of the personal growth and expansion of the awareness of each participant in the process, whether it be a therapeutic endeavor or supervisory consultation.

Bromberg (2013, p. 9), in an extended vignette of his work with a supervisee, illustrates his way of listening to himself and his supervisee simultaneously, and how such dedicated, focused attention to the self-states of each participant brings a fuller awareness of aspects of patient, therapist, supervisee, and supervisor more fully into the work, to the expanded awareness and benefit of all.

Here, as elsewhere, Bromberg's primary attention is to the quality of the therapist's own self-states as they come into awareness and focus as an integral part of the psychoanalytic data that informs his way of listening and the method by which he makes use of what he hears. Bromberg (2013) wrote

> More frequently than we admit, a relational psychoanalysis embodies a therapeutic change in the analyst that goes beyond being a necessary though transient part of what is provided to the patient. In other words, the analyst's change

is, to one degree or another, an actual therapeutic process in which, if things go well, the patient is the therapist's therapist in a way that is not so different from the way the therapist is simultaneously benefiting his patient.

In this vignette Bromberg took note of the gap between Dorothea's (his supervisee) manifestly positive and powerful affective attachment to him, in the absence of an apparently symmetrical experience of his felt connection to her. Bromberg's feelings toward Dorothea were neither mutual nor symmetrical, and that is what caught his attention first. Bromberg described the feeling that there was something "off" about the connection between them, and how that sense of "off-ness" had to be taken seriously as a communication not only about Bromberg and his supervisee, but about Dorothea and her patient as well. It was his recognition of these isomorphic patterns that eventually set him on a path to finding her, Dorothea on a path to finding her patient, and Bromberg and Dorothea to finding a real and generative place to be in the supervision work that they were doing together.

As Bromberg (2013) described

> What was missing was her subjective experience of the process. I kept "waiting" for her to become comfortable enough to share it, or so I told myself. What I did not count on was that while I was "waiting," something was taking place between us dissociately that was making me feel more and more mentally disorganized.

More frequently than we admit, a relational psychoanalysis embodies a therapeutic change in the analyst that goes beyond being a necessary though transient part of what is provided to the patient. In other words, the analyst's change is, to one degree or another, an actual therapeutic process in which, if things go well, the patient is the therapist—patient to me, while presenting "case material" in her official role as her patient's therapist.

Eventually, Bromberg was able to see a different aspect of Dorothea through the use of audiotapes of her sessions:

> that was different from the Dorothea I already knew as a supervisee and I suspected would have been different from the Dorothea her analyst knew as his patient. I was consciously confronted with an anomalous experience of different Dorothea's. But it felt better than "sort-of-knowing" it dissociatively.
>
> The difficulty I was now feeling did not primarily stem from Dorothea's patient, nor even from Dorothea, but from myself. I wanted to experientially connect with both the Dorothea I heard on the tape and the Dorothea who was with me in the here-and-now, and I knew that it required my willingness to contain all aspects of Dorothea and me within an overarchingly creative human relationship.
>
> Dorothea and I could not escape from our dissociative cocoon separately. Something had to take place between us that would lead to something new or Dorothea would remain stuck in the enactment with her patient and I would sink further into my own version of the paralysis that Dorothea felt, being unable to function in either a supervisory or a therapeutic capacity.

Bromberg referred to this process as "the imaginative cocreation of a relational unconscious that makes all this possible when state-sharing becomes possible."

"State-sharing" is a crucial part of the therapeutic process for Bromberg (not just permissible, but necessary), because the therapist's sharing with the patient aspects of their own self-experience as they are able to gain access to it in the patient's presence is often the best and most immediate route to the patient's own dawning awareness of their own dissociated states. This, of course, is no easy task for the therapist, as their gaining access to mental states of their own that have been dissociated does not occur in a pain and anxiety free sphere. On the contrary, it is personally challenging work that puts the therapist in touch with the same kinds of anxiety, dread, and vulnerability that the patient may be experiencing, and so allows them to "know the patient from the inside out" (Bromberg, 1991).

Like Bromberg, clearly informed by his emphasis in the many years of consultative work that we did together with the shared and co-created unconscious and the mutually dissociative field of experience in which the work takes place in mind, I too direct my attention to the extent possible to my own shifting self-states and kaleidoscopic self-experience in the presence of my patient or supervisee (Bass, 2014). Awareness of such states has often gone missing from my, their, and our joint awareness in the presence of one another as we work. I do my best to bring my attention to my own states of mind and body, and take note when it is especially difficult to do so, or when I can feel a drift away from myself that I sense is implicated in my ways of being with and relating to my patient.

Do I feel sleepy in the presence of my patient? Bored? Do I notice in myself states of reverie that take me by surprise, or memories that arrive from sources at first unknown, but which upon further reflection provide me with hints about what my own unconscious or dissociated states have detected about my patient's states of mind, even as I realize that a part of me has been dedicated to avoiding knowing about it?

This way of working (Bromberg, 1991) had its origins in Ferenczi's 1932 Clinical Diary (Dupont, 1988). There Ferenczi described in detail his discovery that difficulties arise from not taking as real the splitting of the personality. Ferenczi acknowledged in that work that even he himself, the pioneer who discovered and theorized such phenomena of split and fragmented selves brought about through trauma, had difficulty fully believing his own findings.

> Apparently I have difficulty really believing that this allegedly split off part is not somehow aware of the things we have discussed openly … The patient knows nothing of what I have told her in an alternative state.
>
> (1988, p. 63)

I (AB), having taken Ferenczi's lessons to heart in my own work with patients who had experienced severe trauma, and aided by my weekly consultations with Bromberg, continued to be surprised and to learn more about the presence of split-off fragments of a person, and the knowledge that they may hold sequestered from other, more familiar parts of themselves from a patient that I discussed in detail in previous writing (Bass, 2001), informed by consultation between 1999 and 2001. Wendy (my patient) had demonstrated intuitive gifts in our therapy that were so extreme that they might warrant being called special "psychic powers." These, as we discovered, included a seemingly uncanny way of knowing things about me that felt truly mystifying at the time, as they tuned in to aspects of my experience that I had no awareness that I was broadcasting. Bromberg (2012) himself described such unusual forms of intersubjective knowing that are familiar to many analysts, citing Elizabeth Lloyd Mayer's (2007) work on anomalous ways of knowing. Bromberg, describing Mayer's research, wrote that these findings "could well hold the future of psychoanalysis between its covers," because ways of knowing beyond what we consider rational are central to intersubjective psychoanalytic work, informing how we come to know our patients, and they us, in ways that take us beyond what we had previously known about our knowing.

My patient had an ambivalent relationship to her "special powers," which she mostly kept to herself, exercising them privately, even secretly, with a sense of dread that they would tell her more than she would want to know, and that if someone else saw her knowing what she knew, they would think that she was either crazy, or a witch. She often experienced her special knowledge as "intrusive thoughts," insisting on telling her something that had happened or would happen, whether she wanted to know it or not. It might be more accurate to say that she felt under the control of these powers, rather than "exercising them," since she didn't usually choose to apply them intentionally. Rather she seemed to be "visited" with information about people that she "should not know," and which frequently frightened her even when what she "saw coming" was relatively benign, because she felt her knowledge as a kind of haunting, as though her ghosts were whispering in her ears. We (together) speculated that there was a part of her that she didn't know who knew things that she did not want to know, but seemed inclined to tell her anyway, "whether she liked it or not." If she tried not to listen, they were likely to show up in a dream, transgressing any boundaries she tried to erect in their way by getting "through the cracks" when her guard was literally down, as she slept.

She was in equal measure (privately) pleased with herself, confident of what she "knew" and frightened when she found that she knew more than she wanted to know or believed she could rationally know about others, especially when her knowledge delivered "bad news." A dream anticipated her husband's cancer, for example, even the afflicted organ. In that case there was good and bad news—as the cancer was serious but her insistence on his getting checked after her dream brought some good news too, as surgery was still possible, extending his life by several years. As we began to explore the origins of her "talent," as we sometimes referred to it in "air quotes," reflecting her ambivalence about it and the fact that she typically didn't own the knowledge as her own, what began to emerge were hazy recollections (or were they dreams?, she wondered?) of incest with her grandfather; as she put it, she had never really forgotten these incidents, but at the same time never really known, because they existed in a state in her that was not subject to "normal" language or "normal memory," in her ways of thinking at the time of what constituted the realm of the normal.

As we came to be able to talk about these experiences in greater detail, she came to think that she had developed the ability to sense her grandfather's state of mind at a distance, to know what he would be expecting of her, whether he would be coming to her for a strange, scary creepy kind of touching, or for something more "grandfatherly." As these "memories" came to her, other strange and terrifying dream-like images appeared in her mind as well—of buried babies—she could not say whether they were alive or dead, or her relationship to them. "Had she killed a baby? she asked in a trance-like intonation in one session. Or "was I the baby that was buried or killed?"

She did carry with her an increasingly firm conviction that her childhood had been prematurely curtailed by the visits from her grandfather, and so the killing of her baby self began to make more sense to her, as a symbolic representation of the ways in which she had been killed at an early age, bringing the premature end of her childhood, while also obstructing a natural transition into adulthood, leaving her with a feeling of being neither a child nor an adult, but caught in between.

As we talked about her special gifts (and the special burdens that came with them) she could increasingly think about these images, to wonder whether they were *really* "memories" or not and seemingly, as a result, there was a sense of being more fully present in trauma states that were becoming increasingly real. This meant that they came with a greater feeling of trust in her own mind, and mine as well, that something had really happened that these images represented and portrayed. She was increasingly able to link them up to her early experiences before and during what she now thought of more clearly as "the incest years," as images led to associations, and her associations led to what she could now say with greater convictions were actually memories of childhood events.

Sometimes, though, our visiting these places that had been cordoned off in a part of her mind that had not been accessible before was too much: she would become flooded with feelings that the returning memories or images were bringing along with them like detritus suspended in a giant wave, and she would appear to "go under" into a trance state in search of the felt sense of safety and the relief of dissociation. At those times, it felt like we had lost contact with whatever we seemed to be coming to know about together before the trance took hold. When this happened I would find sometimes that my own grip on consciousness would loosen as well, as I would notice I was losing track of what she was saying and of what I was thinking. I recall some occasions in which I felt dizzy and worried that I might faint or get sick. I would grip my chair tightly in hope of remaining present and steady.

As she began to experience intense, sometimes unbearable feelings about what she knew and what she couldn't trust that she knew, what she could bear knowing and not bear, and what she could bear my knowing about her with her, I began to experience gaps in my own consciousness during sessions. I was having my own experience of finding out what I could bear witness to, and what I could not bear being present for. It seemed that we were enacting an aspect of her early abandonment by those (her mother in particular) who might have helped if they could bear to stay with her, and know what some part of her must have known about her (her mother's) own father, the perpetrator of abuse on her daughter?

Her long silences and trance-like intonations heralded my own confused mental states, which, after much struggle to find their source in myself, and then in her (I eventually came to describe these states to my patient, what Bromberg referred to above as state-sharing), led us to identify a number of distinct trance-like self-states in my patient—each operating independently and seemingly, as we would find, without conscious awareness of one another. One of these states was associated with late night binge eating, after which she would wake up in the morning seeing evidence of her feast, but without recollection. Another was associated with waking dream states, in which she would enter a dream as she told it in a session, and continue to dream it in my presence, describing the disturbing images in real time, from a state in-between sleep and wakefulness.

The initial discovery of such multiple state phenomena took place during one session when, after a long silence, I shook myself out of the intense hold of vivid hypnogogic imagery when I realized with a start I was on the edge of sleep to ground myself by asking her about a curious statement she had made what seemed like about 10 minutes earlier (though I couldn't be sure that my sense of time was reliable) in an unfamiliar tone about a particularly unusual use of food for generating altered states of consciousness, the last thing I remembered in the session. She became agitated when she realized that she had no recollection of that conversation to which I referred, or of the phenomenon to which I was referring. I was as stunned as she was. Her amnesia for the conversation raised a question in my own mind about the reliability of my own memory, and sense of reality, when my patient commented that she was under the impression that she had spent the entire session in silence, which she had regarded as a first for us. She had taken note of the long silence, but not of the conversation that I believed had preceded it.

Was it possible that I dreamt the part of the session to which I referred to my patient, that I hadn't actually succeeded in keeping myself awake when I thought that I was managing to fight off the pull toward sleep? Had I dreamt being awake? This sense of being unclear as to whether what I remembered was "real experience" or dream images mirrored the state of confusion about reality that my patient lived in much of the time, and we were able to compare notes on this state of confusion over these states of uncertainly in due time.

But in that moment, after a period of intense anxiety (that we shared), in which she wondered for the first time (or at least said it out loud for the first time) if she might be suffering from multiple personality disorder (could one part of her have been speaking, another part of her oblivious to what she said or somewhere else entirely?), she became interested in seeing if it could be possible to bridge gaps between some of these altered states and make use of her uncanny powers of perception in ways that could feel accessible to more of her all at once. In the sessions that followed in which she came to see that there was more of her than met her eye, or any given "I" that she inhabited at the time, we both began to see that she was developing her own radar for probing the rich internal layers of color underlying the monotone she presented to the outside world, and, as she discovered and unveiled her own palette, her speaking voice began to take on a new, firmer, and more direct quality, losing its singsong lilt.

She began to find new ways to harness her talents and intuitive gifts—broadcasting in a fuller range of intonation to express the nuances of what was becoming a more manifestly discerning mind, no longer forced into hiding. As a result, she began to sustain more of a sense of grounding over time, and could begin to face a good deal more of what had happened to her in an increasingly sustained way. This allowed her to make more sense of some of what she knew about her mother, and her grandfather, which had to that point existed and had been expressed only in a trancelike, ethereal voice and state of mind, and in enacted dimensions in which she lived the life of someone who put a lot of her psychic energy into anticipating what dangers were "coming down the hall," and what she could do to stay out of the way of what was coming (finding a way to avoid the worst of it by dissociating). She had been living her trauma for all of these years, rather than remembering the particulars of it beyond the vague outlines that she had access to as she transitioned from dream or trance states to wakeful states of consciousness.

Sometimes it is the patient who brings the therapist's attention to a self-state that is in play, while out of the therapist's awareness, and the patient's too. When strong, trauma-derived dissociation is active in psychotherapeutic work, as Bromberg has vividly portrayed, it often exercises a strong force that holds both participants in its grip unawares, characterized by a sense of being stuck, or lifeless until feelings are freed, set back in motion, which often occurs when enactments serve the function of "waking up" one or the other of the participants from states of reverie, trance, or dissociation.

For example, a therapist described that she had drifted off in a state of reverie as her patient (Anna) told her a story that she had heard many times before, in the exact same words and intonation. Hearing the story again and again had the quality for her of a powerful trance induction, as she quickly fell into its grip. Anna didn't seem to have any idea that she had told her therapist the story again and again. Since the therapist knew exactly what the story would be, and how it would be told, it freed her to drift off into a comforting reverie of her own. It hadn't occurred to her to inquire about the function of the retelling, or to share her experience of it, though she recognized with some curiosity that she would have been able to do that with a different patient. In this case, though, she hadn't been able to find a way to make the fact of the repetition ("are you aware that you have told me this story before?"), its quality of voice, and its hypnotic cadence a subject of inquiry, or to share the state that it put her into with her patient (state-sharing, as Bromberg describes it).

After a while, in the particular session that the therapist described, she suddenly had the feeling that she had lost track of time, and so didn't know how long the patient had been speaking. A moment later, her patient "suddenly" asked her what she thought of what she had been saying. This was a curve ball that shook her out of her comfortable reverie, since she had never called the question before of how the therapist was relating to her story. Like being startled awake from a dream by an alarm clock and trying to bring back the dream, she tried to gather her thoughts. She sensed with some dawning panic that Anna, unbeknownst to her, had moved off from the familiar story she was telling, unaccompanied by the therapist who was lost in her own thought, leaving her patient to her own devices. She had missed the abrupt turn of the patient's mind because she was so familiar with the route that they had traveled so many times before, and figured that she would "catch up with her later."

In that moment, the therapist was brought back to full focused attention on the session with a start, as she tried to capture the elusive threads of the reverie that she had been immersed in to see if they might help. This effort was hampered by the arrival of an unwelcome but familiar feeling of shame that she had lost track of her patient as her mind wandered, as she experienced a sharp jolt of anxiety concerning how she would handle what she expected to be the patient's punitive response to her lapse when she realized that her therapist had stopped listening. The anticipated punishing response that she anticipated had points of reference in both the patient's history and the therapist's, as they both had parents who demanded a lot of attention from their children, and would become hurt and angry when it lapsed or was insufficient, while their parents' attention to their children fell far short of such a standard. The therapist was aware of an impulse to cover up her lack of attention with something out of a therapist's bag of tricks (like, "tell me what comes to your mind," or "how do you imagine I responded to what you just said"), but realized that that would constitute a repetition of Anna's early experiences of gaslighting in which the patient's experience of parental neglect, a repetition of the neglect that her mother had experienced from her own parent as well as from her child, was handled in a way that would likely further shame the patient, who would once again have the experience of not being able to hold another's interest. It appeared that therapist and patient had found their way to enact a scene from each of their childhoods in which repetitions of neglect and shame were central and searingly vivid.

The therapist realized in that moment, in the way one might recover a dream that had been elusive in relation to an association that opens a portal to its dawning awareness, that her moving away from the patient as she did took the form of a reverie of another patient who was angry with her for "not getting her," and had recently broached the topic of termination of her therapy.

When she realized where her mind had gone, she was able to wonder whether she was angry with A for her repetitive story telling. Had she experienced the repetitions as a form of neglect in its own right, denoting that the patient dropped her connection to the therapist in not realizing that she had told her the story many times before? Or did the enactment reveal ways that her patient was angry with *her*, assuming (in a dissociated haze, she assumed) that she (the therapist) had not really been listening, and so she would tell her the same story over and over until she finally heard it? What would it have been like for therapist *and* patient if the therapist had found her way to come out of her own dissociative state to be able to say, "I notice you are telling me the story again in a way that suggests that you don't remember telling me, or don't think I heard it or will remember that you told me." Was one of them (therapist or patient) thinking about bringing their relationship to a close, her association to her other patient offering a kind of dissociated hint about something taking place between the lines of the repetitive story that had initiated this moment in which the therapist had been "caught?"

Had the therapist herself enacted a momentary ending to the therapy, at least in that moment, by leaving the patient to her own devices, or had the patient ended the therapy through a kind of filibuster of repetitions that "terminated" the therapist's ability to think?

As her thoughts now began to generate new links to the patient in front of her, instead of covering over her lapse of attention with one or another psychoanalytic feint (as, for example "why do you ask now what I think?"), the therapist acknowledged that her mind had wandered before the patient asked her to comment on what she had said. Had her patient perhaps noticed that her attention had wandered, pointing out the lapse by quizzing her about "what she thought?"

Her patient at first expressed her anger at "being dropped," in response to which the therapist apologized for her lapse. But she was also able to express interest in what had happened—to both of them in what had just occurred. Had the patient noticed her therapist's state of reverie, or the drift in her attention before interrupting her own story to ask what she had been thinking? Anna acknowledged that she had had a sense that her mind had wandered, from the look in her eyes and, rather than ask about it directly (which she felt too ashamed to do), asked the therapist what she thought, in part as a kind of trap, outing the therapist's neglect, and locating any shame that would surface in the therapist instead. As the presence of shame was now identified in both participants, moving from an enacted dimension to one that they could consider, the therapist was now able to express genuine curiosity about her patient's repetitions, and Anna got in touch with a feeling, unthought until now, that she never really felt that anyone truly listened to her, and that some part of her had hoped that she (her therapist) would have said, "yes, you know you told me about that before, do you remember? do you think I might have forgotten about it," which thought brought tears to her eyes, as it expressed a hidden longing that someone would want to find her. The therapist shared more about what she could locate of her own self-state in that moment, including her sense of Anna's implicit criticism of her in the ways that the patient had denied and projected onto her in her own way of gaslighting. But with the identification and sharing of this feeling came something new— with the recognition that both patient and therapist were both in hiding while also hoping to be found (Winnicott, 1965), therapist and patient were able to find their way back to a sense of connection to themselves and each other. Bromberg emphasized that such forms of state sharing, a kind of self-revelation of the therapist's states of mind in the presence of the patient, is not only permissible in analysis, but necessary, as a way of approaching aspects of the patient's, and analyst's experience, that have been dissociated and enacted to that point (2006a, 2006b).

With his deep appreciation of the ways in which patient and therapist alike occupy a multiplicity of self-states over the course of therapy, and frequently in a single session, Bromberg emphasized that a central part of the analyst's job is to find words to get his own experience of enacted experience into his mind and out on the table in a manner that facilitates the patient's ability to do the same. Such formulation and communication of experience that comes to be understood as "enacted" is necessary because it has existed in a dissociated cocoon that has not been accessible to awareness or symbolization in a primarily verbal dimension in which its meaning is accessible to the patient, or the therapist, and has therefore been inaccessible to awareness or communication in a verbal register.

As Bromberg (1991) described, the patient lives his internal life in therapy, and the enacted dimension in which it is expressed frequently precedes its representation in words, as the latter requires greater self-awareness and a capacity for the symbolization of experience than is available at the times of its representation in an enacted form. In this regard, he referred to Khan's (1971) work in which he wrote:

> The person is all the elements of his dissociated states and lives them as such. It is for the analyst operating as an auxiliary ego … to register these dissociations and help the patient to integrate them into a coherent totality of experience.
>
> (p. 245)

Bromberg showed that the arrival of a patient inhabiting a different self-state from one that the therapist is familiar with, or changing self-states during the course of a session, offers an opportunity, when noted by the therapist, to respond to the "new" patient in the room with some form of direct or indirect acknowledgment of her or his presence and welcome. Such changes in state can be subtle, and are often brought to the therapist's attention by a dawning awareness of a shift in his own state, as we saw in the case of Wendy (p. 81, above).

The recognition of a new presence in the patient may be carried in the tone of the therapist who has taken note of a "visitor" to the session who speaks in a different idiom, or tone, or displays a different kind of body language or posture, or who offers a different point of view, or unfamiliar affect. Sometimes the patient seems to embody a different age or state of development subliminally, without announcing its presence in ways that can be easily apprehended or described.

When the therapist recognizes a different presence in the session, its welcoming acknowledgment can encourage its further elaboration by that part of the patient that has made its appearance, and thus facilitate its further individuation as a voice in the therapy that can become more comfortable and informative over time, as to what part of the patient's experience it has held, including memories, and its relation to other parts of the patient or voices that have been more present in the therapy to that point.

Bromberg has emphasized (1991) that the arrival of a "person," reflecting different (often dissociated) parts of the patient than have had a recognizable voice in the therapy before, offers the therapist an opportunity to begin to get to know a part of the patient who may have been living in isolation, dissociated from other parts, in the shadow of trauma and in so doing invites more of the patient into the fold of what they regard as "me." As the therapist comes to be increasingly able to recognize and come to know different isolated parts of the patient in their own right, the patient comes to be more familiar with different parts of themselves as well, and over time is able to occupy a place in between, from which it is possible to recognize that these are all "parts of me." When the parts of a self that can be identified as "me" rather than "not-me" states that are unrecognizable as part of the self that I know myself to be, shame-based dissociation is diminished as the patient feels an increasing sense of wholeness in the presence of the therapist, and beyond.

Bromberg refers to this developmental achievement as developing the ability to "stand in the spaces (1996) between these different parts. For example, Rob, whom I discussed briefly in Chapter 5 in the context of the paradox of technique in relation to multiplicity of self-experience(s), is a patient whom I had been seeing in analysis for several years at the time of the session I will now describe. He has had a long career in business in which he has been successful, both financially and in terms of the regard of his colleagues, though he often doubts his own competence and feels discouraged and ashamed that he is not "really" measuring up to what is expected of him, and what he expects of himself. He feels that his successful career should come with an "asterisk" attached, that he is not truly the successful person he purports to be. His father, as I have described earlier, had experienced a "reversal of fortune" when he was a young man, when Rob was a nine-year-old boy.

His father quite suddenly and mysteriously (to Rob) lost his powerful and respected professional position. There was never a clear explanation for what had happened, at least one that was offered to his young son, or his slightly older sister. He recalled that his mother's message to the children about what had happened to his father was that it had been a "terrible misunderstanding." He hadn't done anything wrong, and was being unfairly treated. Rob's recollection was that there was little talk of the incident or its impact on the family beyond that (for example, there was no discussion of what the misunderstanding was), notwithstanding the fact that the atmosphere at home changed dramatically. Shortly thereafter his father left home, without any warning or discussion that he could recall, to "get training in a new profession." At first he would visit on weekends. But before long, his parent's marriage began to falter, his father staying at home less and less. Eventually they divorced. Rob recalled a moment from his childhood in which he came home from school to find his mother upset and tearful. He recalled feeling that he surprised her with his presence because she seemed startled by his appearance, though he had come home from school at the usual time.

He had the feeling that his mother had forgotten him in her preoccupation, which he remembered as he spoke about it. making him feel lonely and ashamed of his status as an unexpected, unmemorable, unwanted interloper. He asked his mother what was wrong, as she appeared to be very upset. He felt stunned—mystified and further shamed at her response—"you are." He felt confused, "I was what was wrong? Was I responsible for my father's fall and my mother's misery?"

They never talked about the moment again. Did the moment actually happen, or had he dreamt it, he wondered? He was not sure. But the image, whatever it was (real, fantasized, dreamt, or condensed into the image, constructed as a "screen memory" out of the many moments that carried a sense of the shame of being forgotten and his confusion and mystification at the suggestion that he was responsible for what was going), was etched in his memory and implicated, as we came to see in his chronic feeling that something was about to go wrong in his life that would change things forever, and that he would never know why. Sometimes it took the form of a feeling that he was about to be fired from his job, notwithstanding his success and the good job reviews he received each year.

He could never identify the transgression or the nature of the failure that would lead to his undoing, other than to recognize that the scene of abject humiliation that played over and over in his mind looked a lot like how his father's life had unfolded in reality. When he imagined such scenes filling in the details of his undoing, there would often be a kind of relief that came with it: "at last I will be discovered and found wanting. Maybe then I will be able to relax." I noticed the double entendre in his being "found wanting," and said that some relief might come finally, being recognized in wanting and needing something for himself. He had a feeling that if he got the failing over with, and if he could be seen for who he really was/felt he would have a chance to "start over."

Over time, in our therapy sessions, I began to identify the appearance and presence of the young boy of about nine in the man who was my patient, when he would begin to express "irrational" anxiety that something was about to go terribly wrong. His sense of dread, guilt, and shame were palpable; he would embody a different, much younger person when such states arrived. My image of this boy began to take shape, like a polaroid picture that I could see developing before my eyes, to the point that I could actually begin to see the boy child version of himself that became more distinct over time, alongside the grownup successful business man that I knew. Sometimes I would have sense of the boy's arrival from something in his look and bearing, and could anticipate the anxious words that would follow before they actually came.

As I came to be able to recognize the boy when he appeared, I would invite him to tell me more of the story from his unique vantage point (as the one who had been there) about what he felt he had done to ruin the "lovely" life his family had had, and about the guilt and shame he had carried all these years for ruining it—because there was something wrong with him. Eventually we found that he could talk about what had happened in the presence of his adult self who it seemed was hearing much of the story for the first time. As he shared more of the story with me and his adult self too, we were all able to understand more about why he believed that the life he had built with hard work and his talents felt so fraudulent and precarious, the precariousness that he had carried with him for all these years in what Bromberg would refer to as a "dissociative cocoon," an island of "incompatible truths." Over time, his adult self was able to be reassuring, and correct some of the distortions he detected in his young boy's self's understanding, filling in some information that he (the adult) had learned later from both his parents, but which seemed to come as news to his dissociative child self.

We will end this chapter with a clinical vignette from Bromberg's (2001) paper, in which he describes an encounter with a part of his patient that he hadn't known was there, and he shares with us (the reader) the beginning of a new relationship with her that came of their mutual recognition in the encounter invited by his speaking to a younger part of her directly. It feels like the right way to end this chapter as we approach the end of our book because just as Philip met a part of his patient in this moment, we want to introduce you to this part of Philip in his own words and voice. We had spent a lot of time in the writing of this book remembering and reliving our time with him, hearing his voice and remembering the forms that our relationships with him took over the time we knew him. For those of you who are meeting Philip here for the first time, we thought it would be fitting to leave you with the sound of his own voice in working in the realm of multiplicity.

* * * *

Bromberg quoting his patient: "I was walking to a restaurant with my father, and he holds my hand in this weird way—he won't let go. I had to pretend I was fixing my hair to remove my hand."

Bromberg speaking for himself: "This was her first concrete association that could potentially shed some light on her hair twirling/pulling. Then, suddenly, in the voice of a preadolescent child, she said, "He never touches Mommy that way. I wonder sometimes if people who see us think I shrunk."

"Who would they see?" I ask her.

Now back in the other voice, "They'd see a 10-year-old girl walking with her father. My husband lives with her most of the time. Most of the time he likes it. But he doesn't like it when I change. He says, 'Why do you have to be different people on different days?'"

"Well, I'm glad I had a chance to meet her," I reply, "even if it was only very briefly."

"Yes," she said pointedly. "She went away again as soon as you asked me to *tell* you about her." A bit dazed as the end of the session approached, I mumbled what I hoped would be a supportive response and a "good" note on which to stop: "Maybe if I talk to her more directly, she will stay longer. Do you think so?"

Naively anticipating that this would be our "marker" for next time, I was shocked when she ignored what I thought were my obvious cues that the time was up, and she began a monologue that seemed nonstop. She began to talk about how afraid she is of offending people at whom she secretly scoffs—people who think that what they say matters to her when it really doesn't. "It's so strange," she went on, "even though some people don't seem to get angry about it. I crash when it's over. I'll go home and binge and vomit."

I felt paralyzed at this point. Even though I felt she was talking about *us* and about what it feels like for her after she leaves sessions, I also wanted to end the session. I kept hoping that if I gave her just a little more time I would think of the "right" thing to say, so I let her go on … and on … and on … hoping against hope that if I didn't stop her before she stopped herself, it would end in the "right" way. Well, I finally abandoned that hope and stopped her ten minutes past the end of the session.

She said, sounding a bit miffed, "I haven't finished yet." I replied, probably sounding a bit contrite, "I know, but our time is up for today, and I'd love for us to have a moment to reflect on what just happened here." She retorted, "I never reflect on what I'm saying when I'm like this." I answered, now a bit more composed, "But later when you get home, a different part of you does think about it—all alone. And then you decide you were horrible and end up bingeing and vomiting." At that moment, something "clicked into place" for me, and I added, "But in a funny way, you only did what I asked you to do, didn't you? Remember when I said, 'Maybe if I talk to *her* more directly, she'll stay longer?' I just didn't expect it to happen *now*! But why wouldn't it?" And then, shifting realities, "After all, you were just being you. 'Longer' means until you've finished, right?" She, stood up, grinned, and left. I breathed a grateful sigh of relief.

Afterwords

As this book began to take shape I have been acutely aware of my engagement with Philip on a daily basis. First, in terms of thinking about his opus—the theoretical elaboration of his ideas, his clinical brilliance, and his sensitivity to traumatic experience. Then as the book started to come to a close I found myself aware of the enormity of his gift to me—in what he taught me and my daily application of it, in my teaching of his work in multiple analytic institutes in New York, Italy, and South America as well as my ongoing study groups which began with the appropriate title *The Bromberg Variations*, a name that Philip enjoyed and felt captured his many contributions.

On a more personal note, I realized how often I am in dialogue with him and how sorely I miss him. Philip read everything I wrote and emboldened me to keep going, he remained a friend and staunch supporter throughout our relationship. As I finished some of the chapters on enactment, I came across the following line, from his chapter *Potholes on the Royal Road* addressing unrelenting enactments in treatment and why they occur:

> the analyst's own repeated efforts to relieve his patient's distress *must fail* (emphasis mine) in order for the analyst to know the patient's experience for what it is. But knowing is not enough; the irreparable must somehow be repaired, and the only way the past-as-present can be repaired is within a relationship that repeats the failure of the past but somehow

DOI: 10.4324/9781003381853-11

does more than repeat it. Something new must occur- something that has to emerge out of what patient and analyst do in an unanticipated way.

(Bromberg, 2006, p. 94)

I remembered a particular moment which to me explains something very dear and important about Philip. On the occasion of his 80th birthday the members of my supervision group, Dr. Debra Rothschild, Dr. Larry Zelnick and I gathered together to think about an appropriate gift for Philip. After much thought and deliberation, and knowing that he was an avid reader of poetry and literature, I suggested getting him the complete Harry Potter books. While my colleagues were skeptical, I knew that Philip would appreciate the fact that the books are about trauma, and the magic of transformation through the reparative nature of relationships. Indeed, Philip loved the books and read all seven of them during that summer. He continued to use them often in his clinical supervision and work. He identified with Harry, and often spoke of horcruxes as self-states of the not-me kind.

Just like as analysts we must fail in order to understand our patient's experience, and together work through and repair trauma in the present, so too in the Harry Potter books, Harry must fail in his battle with Lord Voldermort, fail in order to be able to engage him anew, this time as an adversary who can own his experience and *stand in (all of) the spaces.*

Philip gave generously of himself and his gift to me continues to bloom every day as I sit with my patients, teach, and supervise. And my conversation with him continues.

Velleda C. Ceccoli

* * * *

The past and present wilt—I have fill'd them, emptied them.
And proceed to fill my next fold of the future.
Listener up there! what have you to confide to me?
Look in my face while I snuff the sidle of evening,
(Talk honestly, no one else hears you, and I stay only a minute longer.)

Do I contradict myself?
Very well then I contradict myself,
(I am large, I contain multitudes.)

Walt Whitman (1855), Song of Myself

Philip Bromberg, like Walt Whitman and Bob Dylan (2020), knew (from the inside out) that he, and we, contained multitudes. He had an abiding appreciation for the multitudes that we all carry within, and an ear (he would say, his third ear (Reik, 1948)) finely tuned to all the whispering, barely audible sounds revealing the selves behind the selves that we sense inhabit our selves. Often we sense their whispers as the sounds of the rustlings that our actions produce. Philip was rarely chagrined about his own "contradictions," rather he embraced them.

He could become irritable when one was too sure of who they were, as he believed that he, and each of us, are much more than we can, or even want to know, in any given moment. Knowing too much of what we are made of can be hard to bear, and equally hard to bare, even to oneself, but not knowing is a sure way to keep ourselves separated from ourselves and each other, keeping distance rather than coming close. He developed a theory and a way of practicing psychoanalysis that honored what some people call contradictions, or conflicts, by making a place for each and every part of each of us to create a place in ourselves that can expand to contain our largeness all at once, in all our multiplicity.

Philip and I shared an appreciation of Bob Dylan's lyrics. We sometimes quoted the *Ballad of the Thin Man*, that included the line: "Something is happening here, but you don't know what it is," a thought that analysts, especially of the interpersonal relational tradition that Bromberg identified with, are wont to feel themselves.

Something is always happening that is more than we know at the time, so even as "we don't know what it is," there is always another part of the us with another point of view on the matter, yet to be disclosed.

I am sorry that Philip never got to hear Dylan's song, *I Contain Multitudes* (it came out a month before he died). He recognized Dylan as a fellow traveler in the land of multiplicity. When Dylan discovered the poet Arthur Rimbaud's phrase, "Je est un autre"

("I is another"), in the 1960s he said that the phrase caused bells to go off in his mind. He said in an interview (1997): "I change during the course of a day. I wake and I'm one person, and when I got to sleep I'm certain I'm somebody else. I don't know who I am most of the time. It doesn't even matter to me."

It did matter to Philip who he was, who I was, who his friends and patients were, even as he appreciated that there was always more that we don't know, as he dedicated his life to finding out as much as possible about the multitudes that we each contain.

Whitman's *Song of Myself* (1855) set off bells for Philip, as it did for Dylan, something essential about him that he knew "from the inside out" (2007), which is also how Whitman wrote "Do I contradict myself? Very well then, I contradict myself. (I am large. I contain multitudes)." Like Whitman, Philip embraced his multiplicity, his "multitudes," revealing in his work that what may seem like a contradiction in a person, is better described as a communication from another part of the patient, one that as Winnicott suggested, finds that it is both a joy to be hidden and a disaster not to be found.

Philip's recognition of the multiplicity that we all contain led him to see his patients, as he saw himself, not as bundles of contradictions, but rather as humans whose physical and psychological survival have been made possible by the development of a capacity for dissociation, keeping the different parts of ourselves sequestered when necessary in the face of trauma.

Philip pursued a PhD in English literature in the 1960s, before he changed course to study for a PhD in clinical psychology, before going on to psychoanalytic training. But it wasn't really a change of course, because his love and study of literature never ceased, and continued to enrich his understanding of himself and others. He loved Philip Roth, who he resembled and enjoyed being mistaken for, sometimes granting a request for an autograph, imagining himself to be that Philip. I never knew if Philip's story about granting the request for a Roth autograph was apocryphal or true, but it seems plausible that one of my Philips would have granted the request, and taken pleasure in doing so.

As Philip said, not having seen Dylan's identification with the Indiana Jones part of himself, he was more in touch with

Gertrude Stein (1937) in himself in his daily work as an analyst: less an archeologist than a modernist artist, as he noted that "I seem to find my reality shaped more by Gertrude Stein than by Indiana Jones." Stein (1937, p. 298), commenting about the nature of life and the pursuit of goals, wrote that when you finally get there, "there is no there there." My patients frequently make the same comment. The direct experience of "self-change" seems to be gobbled up by the reality of "who you are" at a given moment, and evades the linear experience of beginning, middle, and end. But linear time does indeed have a presence of its own—like the background ticking of a clock that cannot be ignored for too long without great cost—and it is this paradox that seems to make psychoanalysis feel like a relationship between two people, each trying to keep one foot in the here and now and the other in the linear reality of past, present, and future. Described this way, it sounds like a totally impossible process. If, indeed, "everyone knows that every day has no future to it."

Philip's love of reading poetry and fiction was essential to his psychoanalytic work, always close at hand in his own writing, and his clinical work too, as was evident in the following vignette from *Standing in the Spaces*:

I was in the midst of delivering the "truth" once again, when he said to me, in a tone of benevolent exasperation, "I really want to accept what you are saying about me, because I respect you, but I just can't, and I feel caught between … between … Sylvia and the chiropodist." I exploded with laughter, and when I calmed down and wiped the tears from my eyes, I looked up apprehensively, expecting him to be hurt, shamed, or angry at my response. He was neither. Max looked genuinely bewildered. So, I explained why I was laughing, and told him what the actual expression (Scylla and Charybdis) was. He replied, hesitantly, "What's that?" and I then told him the myth. I found myself unable to omit a single detail. I included Jason and the Argonauts, the Straits of Messina, the monsters, the rocks, the whirlpool, the whole thing. When I had finished, he paused, tellingly, and allowed that he was "immensely appreciative" because, as he put it, "you just told me something I needed to know all my life." I was astounded not only that he could let himself use sarcasm with me, but that he could hear it so clearly. I was also shocked (and slightly embarrassed) at having been so unaware of my shift in role. But I was totally unprepared for the moment, as we spoke, when he suddenly recognized that his remark was not only an act of shaming but was simultaneously an authentic expression of appreciation. He could feel that he had indeed learned something new and that he was excited about it. Max and I had each discovered, by sharing the experience, that being "exposed" in the other's eyes was complex but not traumatic. Max got something more than a lesson in Greek mythology; he got the joke. When we began to laugh at it together and talk about it together, different pieces of Max's reality and different pieces of my reality could start to be negotiated....

In my own way of thinking about it, to one part of him I was his beloved mother (whose name, disappointingly, was not Sylvia) for whom he had to be bright, deferential, and without flaw, already possessing all that he might be expected to know. To another part of him I was the chiropodist—the doctor trying to separate him from his painful "handicap." But in my determination to cure him of his "corns" (his perception of who he "really" is), he hadn't experienced the hope of a "better" reality coming out of our relationship until he made his slip, and I responded with more of my own selves hanging out than I had anticipated. Each of us, in the various self-states that comprised our identities at that moment, unexpectedly made intimate contact and felt acknowledged by the other person ...

For Max, it was a transformational experience, in that he became increasingly free to experiment with multiple ways of being within a single relationship. He began to feel less convinced that he would have to tradeoff his self that was constructed through his relationship with his mother in order to become more fully "his own person"—in this case, a bright guy who didn't have to be ashamed of not knowing everything.

After he retired from practicing clinical psychoanalysis in his eighties, he continued his lifelong project of exploring human psychology through the lens of poetry. His final project, which he spoke about with joy and wonder, was his exploration of the overlap between poetry and human psychology, the force and power of poetry in bringing us into contact with parts of ourselves that we haven't known before. The poet is somehow able to show us what we couldn't see before, even if we sort of knew that it was there. He continued to find more of himself in his last days as he revisited the wisdom of the ancient Greek poets, seeing the wisdom of Homer and Hesiod, as he contemplated the growing nearness of his final days (personal communication, Dr. Anthony Lechich).

Some of Philip's fondest memories were moments in which his mother read to him when he was a small child. His love of those moments were close at hand. He once asked a patient (personal communication) what it was like to be read to by her mother, he could feel her mother's presence by the rapt tilt of her head as he spoke. His finding her mother sitting nearby in the session brought a flow of tears she had not experienced in his presence before.

Like Velleda who got to see another part of Phillip in his love of and identification with Harry Potter, one of my fondest memories of my time with Philip was our reading aloud together, with our friend and fellow supervision group member Anita Herron, these lines from Antoine De Saint Exupery's *The Little Prince*. A patient we were discussing evoked Philip's memory of the passage; he pulled it off his shelf, and we read aloud:

"Come and play with me," the Little Prince proposed. "I'm feeling so sad."

"I can't play with you," the fox said. "I'm not tamed."

"Ah, Excuse me," said the little prince. But upon reflection, he added, "What does tamed mean?"

"It's something that's been too often neglected. It means 'to create ties.'...

"'To create ties'?"

"That's right," the fox said. "For me you're only a little boy just like a thousand other little boys. And I have no need of you. And you have no need of me, either. For you, I'm only a fox like a hundred thousand other foxes. But if you tame me, we'll need each other. You'll be the only boy in the world for me. I'll be the only fox in the world for you ..."

"What do I have to do," asked the little prince.

"You have to be very patient," the fox answered. "First you'll set down a little ways away from me, over there, in the grass. I'll watch you out of the corner of my eye, and you won't say anything. Language is the source of mis-understandings. But day by day, you'll be able to sit a little closer ...."

The next day the little prince returned.

The fox said, "It would be better to return at the same time? For instance, if you came at four in the afternoon, I'll begin to be happy by three. The closer it gets to four, the happier I'll be. By four, I'll be all excited and worried. I'll discover what it costs to be happy! But if you come at any old time, I'll never know when I should prepare my heart ... there must be rites."

Philip spent his long life, returning at the same time every day, knowing that language can be a source of misunderstanding as well as deep connection. He understood that being there every day, year after year, learning to be patient with oneself and the other, and to prepare one's ear to meet someone who is becoming special, makes all the difference in learning to sit just a little closer, and to discover the costs of being happy and sad.

Anthony Bass

Bromberg Bibliography

Books

Standing in the Spaces: Essays on Clinical Process, Trauma, and Dissociation. Hillsdale, NJ: Analytic Press, 1998.

Awakening the Dreamer: Clinical Journeys. Hillsdale, NJ: Analytic Press, 2006.

The Shadow of the Tsunami: And the Growth of the Relational Mind. New York: Routledge, 2011.

Other Works

Bromberg, P. M. (1974). On psychoanalytic training—Introduction: The challenge of self-examination. *Contemporary Psychoanalysis*, 10: 239–241.

Bromberg, P. M. (1979). Interpersonal psychoanalysis and regression. *Contemporary Psychoanalysis*, 15: 647–655.

Bromberg, P. M. (1979). The use of detachment in narcissistic and borderline conditions. *Journal of the American Academy of Psychoanalysis*, 7: 593–600.

Bromberg, P. M. (1979). The schizoid personality: The psychopathology of stability. In L. Saretsky, G. D. Goldman, and D. S. Milman (Eds.), *Integrating Ego Psychology and Object Relations Theory.* Iowa: Kendall/Hunt, pp. 226–242.

Bromberg, P. M. (1980). Empathy, anxiety and reality—A view from the bridge. *Contemporary Psychoanalysis*, 16: 223–236.

Bromberg, P. M. (1980). Sullivan's concept of consensual validation and the therapeutic action of psychoanalysis. *Contemporary Psychoanalysis*, 16: 237–248.

Bromberg, P. M. (1982). The supervisory process and parallel process in psychoanalysis. *Contemporary Psychoanalysis*, 18: 92–110.

Bromberg, P. M. (1983). The mirror and the mask: On narcissism and psychoanalytic growth. *Contemporary Psychoanalysis*, 19: 359–387.

Bromberg, P. M. (1984). Getting into oneself and out of one's self: On schizoid processes. *Contemporary Psychoanalysis*, 20: 439–447.

Bromberg, P. M. (1984). The third ear. In L. Caligor, P. M. Bromberg, and J. D. Meltzer (Eds.), *Clinical Perspectives on the Supervision of Psychoanalysis and Psychotherapy*. New York: Plenum Press, pp. 29–44.

Bromberg, P. M. (1984). On the occurrence of the Isakower phenomenon in a schizoid disorder. *Contemporary Psychoanalysis*, 20: 600–624.

Bromberg, P. M. (1986). Discussion of "The Wishy-Washy Personality" by Arnold Goldberg. *Contemporary Psychoanalysis*, 22: 374–386.

Bromberg, P. M. (1989). Discussion of "Keeping the analysis alive and creative" by Gloria Friedman. *Contemporary Psychoanalysis*, 25: 337–345.

Bromberg, P. M. (1991). Artist and analyst. *Contemporary Psychoanalysis*, 27: 289–299.

Bromberg, P. M. (1991). Introduction to symposium: "Reality and the analytic relationship." *Psychoanalytic Dialogues*, 1: 8–12.

Bromberg, P. M. (1991). On knowing one's patient inside out: The aesthetics of unconscious communication. *Psychoanalytic Dialogues*, 1: 399–422.

Bromberg, P. M. (1991). Reply to discussion by Enid Balint. *Psychoanalytic Dialogues*, 1: 431–437.

Bromberg, P. M. (1992). The difficult patient or the difficult dyad? Some basic issues. *Contemporary Psychoanalysis*, 28: 495–502.

Bromberg, P. M. (1993). Discussion of "Obsessions and/or obsessionality: Perspectives on psychoanalytic treatment" by Walter E. Spear. *Contemporary Psychoanalysis*, 29: 90–100.

Bromberg, P. M. (1993). Shadow and substance: A relational perspective on clinical process. *Psychoanalytic Psychology*, 10: 147–168.

Bromberg, P. M. (1994). "Speak! That I may see you": Some Reflections On Dissociation, Reality, And Psychoanalytic Listening. *Psychoanalytic Dialogues*, 4: 517–547.

Bromberg, P. M. (1995). Resistance, object-usage, and human relatedness. *Contemporary Psychoanalysis*, 31: 173.

Bromberg, P. M. (1995). Introduction to David E. Schecter's "Attachment, detachment, and psychoanalytic therapy." In D. B. Stern, C. Mann, S. Kantor, and G. Schlesinger (Eds.), *Pioneers of Interpersonal Psychoanalysis*. Hillsdale, NJ: Analytic Press, pp. 169–174.

Bromberg, P. M. (1995). A rose by any other name: Commentary on Lerner's "Treatment issues in a case of possible multiple personality disorder". *Psychoanalytic Psychology*, 12: 143–149.

Bromberg, P. M. (1995). Psychoanalysis, dissociation, and personality organization: Reflections on Peter Goldberg's essay. *Psychoanalytic Dialogues*, 5:511–528.

Bromberg, P. M. (1996). Hysteria, dissociation, and cure: Emmy von N revisited. *Psychoanalytic Dialogues*, 6: 55–71.

Bromberg, P. M. (1996). Standing in the spaces: The multiplicity of self and the psychoanalytic relationship. *Contemporary Psychoanalysis*, 32: 509–535.

Bromberg, P. M. (1997). Commentary on Lawrence Friedman's "Ferrum, ignis, and medicina: Return to the crucible." *Journal of the American Psychoanalytic Association*, 45: 36–40.

Bromberg, P. M. (1998). Staying the same while changing: Reflections on clinical judgment. *Psychoanalytic Dialogues*, 8: 225–236.

Bromberg, P. M. (1998). Introduction. In *Standing in the Spaces: Essays on Clinical Process, Trauma, and Dissociation*. Hillsdale, NJ: Analytic Press, pp. 1–19.

Bromberg, P. M. (1998). Help! I'm going out of my mind. In *Standing in the Spaces: Essays on Clinical Process, Trauma, and Dissociation*. Hillsdale, NJ: Analytic Press, pp. 309–328.

Bromberg, P. M. (1999). Playing with boundaries. *Contemporary Psychoanalysis*, 35: 54–66.

Bromberg, P. M. (2000). Bringing in the dreamer: Some reflections on dreamwork, surprise, and analytic process. *Contemporary Psychoanalysis*, 36: 685–705.

Bromberg, P. M. (2000). Potholes on the royal road: Or is it an abyss? *Contemporary Psychoanalysis*, 36: 5–28.

Bromberg, P. M. (2000). Reply to reviews of "Standing in the spaces: Essays on clinical process, trauma, and dissociation" (Reviewers: Marcia Cavell, Randall Sorenson, and Henry Smith). *Psychoanalytic Dialogues*, 10: 551–568.

Bromberg, P. M. (2001). Hope when there is no hope: Discussion of Jill Schaiff's case presentation. *Psychoanalytic Inquiry*, 21: 519–529.

Bromberg, P. M. (2001). The gorilla did it: Some thoughts on dissociation, the real, and the really real. *Psychoanalytic Dialogues*, 11: 385–404.

Bromberg, P. M. (2001). Treating patients with symptoms and symptoms with patience: Reflections on shame, dissociation, and eating disorders. *Psychoanalytic Dialogues*, 11: 891–912.

Bromberg, P. M. (2002). Speak to me as to thy thinkings: Commentary on "Interpersonal psychoanalysis' radical façade" by Irwin Hirsch. *Journal of the American Academy of Psychoanalysis*, 30: 605–620.

Bromberg, P. M. (2003). On being one's dream: Some reflections on Robert Bosnak's "Embodied imagination". *Contemporary Psychoanalysis*, 39: 697–710.

Bromberg, P. M. (2003). One need not be a house to be haunted: On enactment, dissociation, and the dread of "not-me"—A case study. *Psychoanalytic Dialogues*, 13: 689–709.

Bromberg, P. M. (2003). Something wicked this way comes: Trauma, dissociation, and conflict: The space where psychoanalysis, cognitive science, and neuroscience overlap. *Psychoanalytic Psychology*, 20: 558–574.

Bromberg, P. M. (2004). More than meets the eye: A Professional autobiography. *Psychoanalytic Inquiry*, 24: 558–575.

Bromberg, P. M. and Chefetz, R. A. (2004). Talking with "me" and "not-me": A dialogue. *Contemporary Psychoanalysis*, 40: 409–464.

Bromberg, P. M. (2006). When reality blinks. In P. M. Bromberg, *Awakening the Dreamer: Clinical Journeys*. Hillsdale, NJ: Analytic Press, pp. 1–27.

Bromberg, P. M. (2006). Bringing in the dreamer. In P. M. Bromberg, *Awakening the Dreamer: Clinical Journeys*. Hillsdale, NJ: Analytic Press, pp. 31–50.

Bromberg, P. M. (2006). The analyst's "self-revelation": Not just permissible but necessary. In P. M. Bromberg, *Awakening the Dreamer: Clinical Journeys*. Hillsdale, NJ: Analytic Press, pp. 128–150.

Bromberg, P. M. (2006). "Ev'ry time we say goodbye, I die a little ...:" Commentary on Holly Levenkron's "Love (and hate) with the proper stranger". *Psychoanalytic Inquiry*, 26: 182–201.

Bromberg, P. M. (2006). It never entered my mind: Some reflections on desire, dissociation, and disclosure. In J. Petrucelli (Ed.), *Longing: Psychoanalytic Musings on Desire*. London: Karnac Books, pp. 13–23.

Bromberg, P. M. (2007). Reply to reviews of "Awakening the dreamer: Clinical journeys" by Philip M. Bromberg (Reviewers: Ethel Person, Susan Sands, and Allan Schore). *Psychoanalytic Dialogues*, 17: 769–787.

Bromberg, P. M. (2007). Response to reviews of "Awakening the dreamer: Clinical journeys" (Reviewers: Jessica Benjamin, Max Cavitch, and Robert Langan). *Contemporary Psychoanalysis*, 43: 696–708.

Bromberg, P. M. (2007). The analytic moment doesn't fit analytic "technique:" Commentary on Tony Bass's "When the frame doesn't fit the picture". *Psychoanalytic Dialogues*, 17: 909–921.

Bromberg, P. M. (2008). "Grown-up" words: An interpersonal/relational perspective on unconscious fantasy. *Psychoanalytic Inquiry*, 28: 131–150.

Bromberg, P. M. (2008). Mentalize THIS!: Dissociation, enactment, and clinical process. In E. Jurist, A. Slade, and S. Bergner (Eds.), *Mind to*

Mind: Infant Research, Neuroscience, and Psychoanalysis. New York: Other Press, pp. 414–434.

Bromberg, P. M. (2008). Shrinking the tsunami: Affect-regulation, dissociation, and the shadow of the flood. *Contemporary Psychoanalysis*, 44: 329–350.

Bromberg, P. M. (2009). Multiple self-states, the relational mind, and dissociation: A psychoanalytic perspective. In P. F. Dell and J. A. O'Neil (Eds.), *Dissociation and the Dissociative Disorders: DSM-V and Beyond.* New York: Routledge, pp. 637–652.

Bromberg, P. M. (2009). Discussion of Robert Grossmark's "Case of Pamela". *Psychoanalytic Dialogues*, 19: 31–38.

Bromberg, P. M. (2009). Truth, human relatedness, and the analytic process: An interpersonal/relational perspective. *International Journal of Psychoanalysis*, 90: 347–361.

Bromberg, P. M. (2010). Minding the dissociative gap. *Contemporary Psychoanalysis*, 46: 19–31.

Bromberg, P. M. (2010). The nearness of you: Navigating selfhood, otherness, and uncertainty. In J. Petrucelli (Ed.), *Knowing, Not-Knowing and Sort-of-Knowing: Psychoanalysis and the Experience of Uncertainty.* London: Karnac, pp. 22–45.

Bromberg, P. M. (2010). Commentary on Carola M. Kaplan's "Navigating trauma in Joseph Conrad's 'Victory': A voyage from Sigmund Freud to Philip M. Bromberg". *Psychoanalytic Dialogues*, 20: 449–455.

Bromberg, P. M. (2011). The Gill/Bromberg Correspondence. *Psychoanalytic Dialogues*, 21: 243–252.

Bromberg, P. M. (2011). "Afterword" to the Gill/Bromberg correspondence. *Psychoanalytic Dialogues*, 21: 264–267.

Bromberg, P. M. (2011). Shrinking the tsunami. In *The Shadow of the Tsunami: And the Growth of the Relational Mind.* New York: Routledge, pp. 13–36.

Bromberg, P. M. (2011). Minding the dissociative gap. In *The Shadow of the Tsunami: And the Growth of the Relational Mind* New York: Routledge, pp. 67–88.

Bromberg, P. M. (2011). "The nearness of you": A personal book-end. In *The Shadow of the Tsunami: And the Growth of the Relational Mind.* New York: Routledge, pp. 167–186.

Bromberg, P. M. (2012). Stumbling along and hanging-in: If this be technique, make the most of it! *Psychoanalytic Inquiry*, 32: 3–17.

Bromberg, P. M. (2012). Credo. *Psychoanalytic Dialogues*, 22: 273–278.

Bromberg, P. M. (2013). Hidden in plain sight: Thoughts on imagination and the lived unconscious. *Psychoanalytic Dialogues*, 23: 1–14.

Greif, D. and Livingston, R. H. (2013). An interview with Philip M. Bromberg, Ph.D. *Contemporary Psychoanalysis*, 49: 323–355.

Bromberg, P. M. (2014). Introduction to "WE" by Aurelia Levi. *Contemporary Psychoanalysis*, 50: 298–300.

Bromberg, P. M. (2014). Sullivan as pragmatic visionary: Operationalist and OperRelationalist. *Contemporary Psychoanalysis*, 50: 509–530.

Bromberg, P. M. (2017). Psychotherapy as the growth of wholeness: The negotiation of individuality and otherness. In M. Solomon and D. Siegel (Eds.), *How People Change*. New York: Norton, pp. 17–52.

Bromberg, P. M. (2017). Reflections on the concept of a traumatic field. In J. Petrucelli and S. Schoen (Eds.), *Unknowable, Unspeakable, and Unsprung: Psychoanalytic Perspectives on Truth, Scandal, Secrets, and Lies*. New York: Routledge, pp. 33–41.

References

Bass, A. (2001). It takes one to know one; or, whose unconscious is it anyway? *Psychoanalytic Dialogues*, 11: 683–670.

Bass, A. (2014). Supervision and analysis at a crossroad: The development of the analytic therapist: Discussion of papers by Joan Sarnat and Emanuel Berman. *Psychoanalytic Dialogues*, 24: 540–548.

Bass, A. (2015). The dialogue of unconsciouses, mutual analysis and the uses of the self in contemporary relational psychoanalysis. *Psychoanalytic Dialogues*, 25: 2–17.

Benjamin, J. (2007). Review of *Awakening the dreamer: Clinical journeys*, by Philip Bromberg. *Contemporary Psychoanalysis*, 43: 666–680.

Bollas, C. (1983). Expressive uses of the countertransference: Notes to the patient from oneself. *Contemporary Psychoanalysis*, 19: 1–33.

Bromberg, P. M. (1973). [ch2]

Bromberg, P. M. (1979a). Interpersonal psychoanalysis and regression. *Contemporary Psychoanalysis*, 15: 647–655.

Bromberg, P. M. (1979b). The schizoid personality: The psychopathology of stability. In L. Saretsky, G. D. Goldman, and D. S. Milman (Eds.), *Integrating Ego Psychology and Object Relations Theory: Psychoanalytic Perspectives On Psychopathology*. Dubuque, IA: Kendall/Hunt Publishing Company, pp. 226–242.

Bromberg, P.M. (1980a). Empathy, anxiety and reality: A view from the bridge. *Contemporary Psychoanalysis*, 16: 223–236.

Bromberg, P.M. (1980b). Sullivan's concept of consensual validation and the therapeutic action of psychoanalysis. *Contemporary Psychoanalysis*, 16: 237–248.

Bromberg, P. M. (1984). The third ear. In L. Califor, P. M. Bromberg, and J. D. Meltzer (Eds.), *Clinical Perspectives on the Supervision of Psychoanalysis and Psychotherapy*. New York: Plenum Press, pp. 29–44.

Bromberg, P. M. (1991). On knowing one's patient inside out: The aesthetics of unconscious communication. *Psychoanalytic Dialogues*, 1: 399–422.

Bromberg, P. M. (1993). Shadow and substance: A relational perspective on clinical process. *Psychoanalytic Dialogues*, 10: 147–168.

Bromberg, P. M. (1994). "Speak! That I may see you": Some reflections on dissociation, reality, and psychoanalytic listening. *Psychoanalytic Dialogues*, 4: 517–547.

Bromberg, P. M. (1995). Introduction to David Schecter's attachment, detachment in psychoanalytic therapy. In D. B. Stern, et al. (Eds.), *Pioneers of Interpersonal Psychoanalysis*. Hillsdale, NJ: Analytic Press, pp. 169–190.

Bromberg, P. M. (1996). Standing in the spaces: The multiplicity of self and the psychoanalytic relationship. *Contemporary Psychoanalysis*, 32: 509–535.

Bromberg, P. M. (1998a). "Speak! That I may see you": Some reflections on dissociation, reality, and psychoanalytic listening. In *Standing in the Spaces: Essays On Clinical Process, Trauma and Dissociation*. Hillsdale, NJ: Analytic Press, pp. 241–266. (Original work published 1994).

Bromberg, P. M. (1998b). Standing in the spaces: The multiplicity of self and the psychoanalytic relationship. In *Standing in the Spaces: Essays On Clinical Process, Trauma and Dissociation*. Hillsdale, NJ: Analytic Press, pp. 267–290. (Original work published 1996).

Bromberg, P. M. (1998c). *Standing in the Spaces: Essays on Clinical Process, Trauma and Dissociation*. Hillsdale, NJ: Analytic Press.

Bromberg, P. M. (2000). Potholes on the royal road: Or is it an abyss? *Contemporary Psychoanalysis*, 36: 5–28.

Bromberg, P. M. (2001a). Treating patients with symptoms and symptoms with patience: Reflections on shame, dissociation, and eating disorders. *Psychoanalytic Dialogues*, 11: 891–912.

Bromberg, P. M. (2001b). The gorilla did it: Some thoughts on dissociation, the real, and the really real. *Psychoanalytic Dialogues*, 11: 385–404.

Bromberg, P. M. (2006a). *Awakening the Dreamer: Clinical Journeys*. Mahwah, NJ: The Analytic Press.

Bromberg, P. M. (2006b). The analyst's "self-revelation" not just permissible, but necessary. In P. M. Bromberg, *Awakening the Dreamer*. Mahwah, NJ: The Analytic Press, pp. 128–150.

Bromberg, P. M. (2008). Shrinking the tsunami: Affect regulation, dissociation, and the shadow of the flood. *Contemporary Psychoanalysis*, 44: 329–350.

Bromberg, P. M. (2011). *The Shadow of the Tsunami and the Growth of the Relational Mind*. New York: Routledge.

Bromberg, P. M. (2012a). Credo. *Psychoanalytical Dialogue*, 22 (3): 273–278.

Bromberg, P. M. (2012b). Stumbling along and hanging in: If this be technique, make the most of it! *Psychoanalytic Inquiry*, 32 (1): 3–17.

Bromberg, P. M. (2013). Hidden in plain sight: Thoughts on imagination and the lived unconscious. *Psychoanalytic Dialogues*, 23: 1–14.

Bromberg, P. M. (2014). Sullivan as pragmatic visionary: Operationalist and OperRelationalist. *Contemporary Psychoanalysis*, 50: 509–530.

Bucci, W. (1997a). Patterns of discourse in "good" and troubled hours: A multiple code interpretation. *Journal of the American Psychoanalytic Association*, 45: 155–187.

Bucci, W. (1997b). *Psychoanalysis and Cognitive Science: A Multiple Code Theory*. New York: Guilford Press.

Bucci, W. (2001). Pathways of emotional communication. *Psychoanalytic Inquiry*, 21: 40–70.

Bucci, W. (2003). The referential process, consciousness, and the sense of self. *Psychoanalytic Inquiry*, 22: 766–793.

Bucci, W. (2007a). Dissociation from the perspective of multiple code theory—Part I: Psychological roots and implications for psychoanalytic treatment. *Contemporary Psychoanalysis*, 43: 165–184.

Bucci, W. (2007b). Dissociation from the perspective of multiple code theory—Part II: The Spectrum of dissociative processes in the psychoanalytic relationship. *Contemporary Psychoanalysis*, 43: 305–326.

Bucci, W. (2010). The uncertainty prnciple in the psychoanalytic process. In J. Petrucelli (Ed.), *Knowing, Not-Knowing, and Sort-of Knowing: Psychoanalysis and the Experience of Uncertainty*. London: Karnac, pp. 203–214.

Bucci, W. (2011). The interplay of subsymbolic and symbolic processes in psychoanalytic treatment: It takes two to tangobut who knows the steps, who's the leader? The choreography of the psychoanalytic interchange. *Psychoanalytic Dialogues*, 21 (1): 45–54.

Cavitch, M. (2007). Review of *Awakening the Dreamer*. *Contempoorary Psychoanalysis*, 43 (4): 681–688.

Ceccoli, V. C. (2012). The relational use of self and space in creation: Commentary on paper by Frank Summers. *Psychoanalytic Dialogues*, 22: 178–181.

Chefetz, R. A. & Bromberg, P. M. (2004). Talking with "me" and "not-me": A dialogue. *Contemporary Psychoanalysis*, 40 (3): 409–464.

Cooper, S. H. (2000). Illuminating the shadows in the spaces: A review of *Standing in the Spaces: Essays on Clinical Process, Trauma, and Dissociation* by Philip Bromberg. Hillsdale, NJ: The Analytic Press, 1998. 365 pp. *Contemporary Psychoanalysis*, 36: 143–148.

Dupont, J. (1988). *The Clinical Diary of Sandor Ferenczi.* Cambridge, MA: Harvard University Press.

Dylan, B. (2007). *Dylan on Dylan, the Essential Interviews,* edited by Jonathan Cott. London: Hodder & Stoughton, reprinted from his San Francisco, 1965 press conference.

Dylan, B. (2020). "I Contain Multitudes" (song title) in *Rough and Ready Ways,* Album, Columbia Records.

Edelman, G. M. (1989). *The Remembered Present: A Biological Theory of Books.* New York: Basic Books.

Fonagy, P., Gergely, G., Jurist, E. L., & Target, M. (2005). *Affect Regulation, Mentalization, and the Development of the Self.* New York: Other Press.

Greenberg, J. R., & Mitchell, S. A. (1983). *Object Relations in Psychoanalytic Theory.* Cambridge, MA: Harvard University Press.

Haley, J. (1993). *Jay Haley on Milton H. Erickson.* New York: Brunner/Mazel.

Khan, M. (1971), "To hear with the eyes": Clinical notes on body as subject and object. In M. Khan, *The Privacy of the Self: Papers on Psychoanalytic Theory and Technique.* New York: International Universities Press, 1974, pp. 234–250.

Kihlstrom, J. (1987). The cognitive unconscious. *Science,* 237, 1445–1452.

Lanius, R. (2025). *Sensory Pathways to Healing from Trauma.* New York: Norton.

LeDoux, J. E. (1989). Cognitive-emotional interactions in the brain. *Cognition & Emotion,* 3: 267–289.

LeDoux, J. E. (1994). Emotion, memory, and the brain. *Scientific American,* 270: 32–39.

LeDoux, J. E. (1995). Emotion: Clues from the brain. *Annual Review of Psychology,* 46: 209–235.

LeDoux, J. E. (1996). *The Emotional Brain.* New York: Touchstone.

LeDoux, J. E. (1999). Psychoanalytic theory: Clues from the brain: Commentary. *Neuro-Psychoanalysis,* 1 (1): 44–49.

LeDoux, J. E. (2002). *The Synaptic Self.* New York: Viking.

Levenson, E. A. (1972). *The Fallacy of Understanding.* New York: Basic Books.

Levenson, E. A. (1982). Follow the fox: An inquiry into the vicissitudes of psychoanalytic supervision. *Contemporary Psychoanalysis,* 18 (1): 1–15.

Levenson, E. A. (1983). *The Ambiguity of Change.* New York: Basic Books.

Levenson, E. A. (1991). *The Purloined Self.* New York: Contemporary Psychoanalytic Books.

Mayer, E. L. (2007). *Extraordinary Knowing: Science, Skepticisim, and the Inexplicable Powers of the Human Mind.* New York: Bantam Books.

Mitchell, S. A. (1988). *Relational Concepts in Psychoanalysis.* Cambridge, MA: Harvard University Press.

Mitchell, S. A. (1991). Contemporary perspectives on self: Toward an integration. *Psychoanalytic Dialogues,* 1: 121–147.

Mitchell, S. A. (1993). *Hope and Dread in Psychoanalysis.* New York: Basic Books.

Mitchell, S. A. (2000). *Relationality: From Attachment to Intersubjectivity.* Hillsdale, NJ: Analytic Press.

Putnam, F. W. (1988). The switch process in multiple personality disorder and other state-change disorders. *Dissociation,* 1: 24–32.

Putnam, F. W. (1992). Discussion: Are alter personalities fragments or figments? *Psychoanalytic Inquiry,* 12: 95–111.

Reik, T. (1949). *Listening with the Third Ear: The Inner Experience of a Psychoanalyst.* New York: Farrar, Straus & Giroux.

Schecter, D. (1973). On the emergence of human relatedness. In E. Witenberg (Ed.), *Interpersonal Explorations in Psychoanalysis: New Directions in Theory and Practice.* New York: Basic Books.

Schore, A. N. (1994). *Affect Regulation and the Origin of the Self: The Neurobiology of Emotional Development.* New York: Taylor & Francis.

Schore, A. N. (2003a). *Affect Dysregulation and the Disorders of the Self.* New York: Norton.

Schore, A. N. (2003b). *Affect Dysregulation and the Repair of the Self.* New York: Norton.

Schore, A. N. (2007). Review of *Awakening the dreamer: Clinical journeys,* by Philip M. Bromberg. *Psychoanalytic Dialogues,* 17: 753–767.

Siegel, D. J. (2024). *Personality and Wholeness in Therapy: Integrating 9 Patterns of Development Pathways in Clinical Practice.* New York: Norton.

Stein, G. (1937). *Everybody's Autobiography.* Cambridge, MA: Exact Change, 1993.

Stern, D. N. (1997). *Unformulated Experience: From Dissociation to Imagination in Psychoanalysis.* Hillsdale, NJ: Analytic Press.

Stern, D. N., Bruschweiler-Stern, N., Harrison, A. M., Lyons-Ruth, K., Morgan, A. C., Nahum, J. P., Sander, L., & Tronick, E. Z. (1998). The process of therapeutic change involving iimplicit knowledge: Some implications of developmental observations for adult psychotherapy. *Infant Mental Health Journal,* 19: 300–308.

Stern, D. N. (2009). *Partners in Thought: Working with Unformulated Experience, Dissociation and Enactment.* New York: Routledge.

Sullivan, H. S. (1953). *The Interpersonal Theory of Psychiatry.* New York: Norton.

Whitman, W. (1855). *Leaves of Grass.* Self-published.

Winnicott, D. W. (1965). Communicating and not communicating leading to a study of certain opposites (1963). In *The Maturational Processes and the Facilitating Environment: Studies in the Theory of Emotional Development*, pp. 179–192.

Wolstein, B. (1992). Resistance interlocked with countertransference—R. N. and Ferenczi, and American Interpersonal Relations. *Contemporary Psychoanalysis*, 28: 172–189.

Index